Jim,
Yours in good health!

Confessions of a Repentant
Medical Whore

There Is No Pill For An Unforgiving Heart

JDPD Enterprises, LLC.
PO Box 630605
Nacogdoches, Texas 75963

Cover & Interior design
by Mark Mayfield

Davis, Joe
The Confessions of a Repentant Medical Whore

ISBN 978-0-615-33638-1
Printed in the United States of America, Litho Press Inc.
first Printing December 2009

This is dedicated to Pam; my wife,
my typist, and always present editor and sounding board.

Table of Contents

Acknowledgments

No book is ever written without the assistance of many people. I have been so blessed to have had many wonderful friends and family who have been a part of this process and to whom I am so thankful. To my mother who has always been my biggest fan and most forgiving critic. To Carol Hill, who just could not stand all those contractions. Thanks to Joan Quimby for her patience in copy editing.

Thanks to JR and Patti Russell, Kim Snyder, Jerry and Alice Smith, Mike Stump and Brenda Hill for their time in reading and constructive feedback. To Robyn Gandin for encouraging me to stick with my title. To Rick Hurst and Peter Fagan, physicians and friends who shared their time and who chose to think deeply with me about these issues and provide editorial comments. To Norma Atherton and Sherry Pfaffenberg for encouraging me to write this book. But perhaps most of all, I must thank the patients who God placed in my path and allowed me to share in the intimacy of their lives.

Introduction

Have you ever struggled with a complex problem for days, weeks, or even years and, suddenly, its solution come to you in a flash? And the answer is so simple you don't know how you ever had such trouble figuring out the solution. I'll just bet you have. Many would call this an epiphany. Others, sudden insight.

This book is about several such "epiphanies" that I have experienced over a period of many years, beginning as a student in high school and continuing through college, medical school, internship, residency, fellowship and, finally, thirty-odd years as a practicing - and I do mean practicing - physician of medicine, mostly in a small town in East Texas with a few professional side jaunts along the way.

Once you saw your way clearly through the problem, do you recall how excited you were and how difficult it was to get others to see what you had so clearly seen? You realize that having a vision of the solution and being able to communicate that vision to another is a whole different kettle of fish. Now you have a new problem to mentally tussle with, and that is: Is your idea of a solution just a private epiphany or is it one that just might help someone else who has need of a similar solution to a similar problem?

If you are like I am, you try your idea or ideas out on others. After all, what good is a solution if you are the only one who benefits from solving it? We like confirmation. We like to communicate. Those are just two of the many features of our inherited "socialness." This book has a number of controversial ideas, for which I take full responsibility. Actually, I take full responsibility for my interpretation of these ideas. My interpretation of these ideas is perhaps the controversial part.

Why am I writing this book? The answer to that question, other than the ones listed above, confirmation and communication, is actually one of my epiphanies. I love you, all of you, and I want you to be happy and healthy. Not just occasionally, but all the time. I am writing this book because of my romantic notion that you and I are worth the effort.

A number of people have asked me: "Who is your audience?" Who should read this book? I confess I am a chronic quoter. There have been, and are, a lot of smart and thought-provoking people in this world. Interestingly, the smartest of them never wrote down a word that we know of. He did not have to write down a word because, in fact, He was The Word.

The rest of us are left here on Planet Earth casting our words about, looking for others to communicate with. The following pages contain ideas that I have struggled to put into words for many years. I have borrowed the words of many to help me in my efforts to find those "just right" words to convey my thoughts.

Blaise Pascal, a French mathematician, philosopher and, ultimately, born-again Christian, said this in his Pensées in 1670:

There are only three kinds of persons: those who serve God having found Him; others who are occupied in seeking Him, not having found Him; while the remainder live without seeking Him and without having found Him. The first are reasonable and happy, the last are foolish and unhappy, those between are unhappy and unreasonable.

If you have read Pascal's words and see yourself as one of the three types of persons, then you are my audience. If you read these words and do not see yourself as one of these three types, you are not my audience and will probably not enjoy this book.

If you have picked up this book thinking it contains the salacious details of a doctor and his modern-day hospital peccadillos as portrayed on any number of television series, you will be disappointed. I respect you more than to violate the relationship I seek with you.

I retired from the active hospital practice of medicine a few years ago. Shortly thereafter, my wife and I were on a walk and she asked me: What next? At that time I told her I wasn't sure, but whatever I did, I wanted to communicate with people at a much deeper level. This book is my best attempt to do just that.

I apologize at the outset for the unavoidable autobiographical nature of much of what I offer you. I sincerely hope the end will justify the means.

All of what you will read is true. The conversations that I have recorded may not be exact but are to the best of my recall. It is a book of nonfiction. I have changed the names and occupations of the people and patients out of respect for their privacy.

Perhaps a warning is in order here. This book is about thinking and is intended to make you do so. Although I hope you find it at times entertaining, it is not written with entertainment as its goal. When I told my mother this book was designed to make people think, her comment was, "Jodie, I like to think but sometimes I have to go behind the door to do it."

This book has not been written in haste. I have been writing this book in my mind for at least the last twenty years. My poor wife has patiently listened to these twelve chapters repeatedly in the conversations we have shared as I expressed the ideas contained within them. These ideas have evolved over the last several years as we actively practiced medicine - I as a physician, she as a nurse. She in many ways is glad to see it finally written down on paper.

The actual setting down of these thoughts on paper is an extension of a course I continue to teach at a local church here in our lovely East Texas town. The course I teach is an outgrowth of a series of talks I have given on preventive medicine. Using the *Bible, Guyton's Textbook of Medical Physiology* and *A Course in Miracles,* I believe that we can prevent the vast majority of illnesses to which we humans fall prey.

I do not actually belong to any church, nor am I a certified member of any denomination, but enjoy the process of being what I call a church gadfly. I like to visit. Much to my wife's chagrin, we continue to visit. And visit. One of the things I like about visiting different churches is listening to different presentations of the message. I find myself always in a position of a debater. Do I agree with what is being said? Do I agree with his or her interpretation of scripture? Over the years I have discussed this attitude of mine with my many minister friends, and rather than being upset by the notion, some have actually encouraged me. They encouraged me to think. To think deeply about what Jesus had to say. What was Jesus saying in those red letter parts of the Bible?

Was He in fact just talking to his immediate audience of the ancient Middle East or did He have something to say to us in the "good ole" USA today? Was it practical advice and could it answer some of the very challenging issues we face in our ordinary lives today?

More to the point, what insight could I gather from what he had to say 2000 years ago that would help me, Joe Davis, wrap my mind around our current health care crisis in America?

In the process of debating with Jesus, which I fully admit I continue to do today, I found myself sliding into a relationship with Him that grew deeper and ever more respectful. Respectful of how smart this guy really is. Easily, I can say today, from the perspective of medical science, He was and is the smartest man I have ever met or known.

If you find yourself concerned over the current health care crisis, this book has some good news for you. You are not as sick as you may have been led to believe and help is available, coming from a place you might not have expected.

Let me end this introduction with a summary question of what I want to ask and answer in this book. Let me assure you, the answer is vitally important to each of us in far more ways than you might at this time be inclined to grant. The question?

Would you rather be happy and healthy or would you rather be right?

I die before my time and my body shall be given back to the earth and devoured by worms. What an abysmal gulf between my deep miseries and the eternal Kingdom of Christ. I marvel that whereas the ambitious dreams of myself and of Alexander and Caesar should have vanished into thin air, a Judean peasant - Jesus - should be able to stretch His hands across the centuries, and control the destinies of men and nations.

Napoleon Bonaparte

Chapter 1

The Desire to Be Right

From any tree of the garden you may eat freely; but from the tree of the knowledge of good and evil you shall not eat.
> God to Adam in the garden on the rules of the game.

Further, no man can judge another, because no man knows himself.
> Sir Thomas Browne (1605-1682)
> English physician and writer

I am a practicing internal medicine physician in a small town in East Texas. I have been asked by many people over the years why I became a doctor. Ultimately, there are two main reasons and some minor ones as to why I chose this field.

First, I loved science and I liked people. It did not hurt that the kindly Dr. Hoffmaster, who was our family's doc when I was growing up, drove the neatest Cadillac convertible or that for some strange reason, I have always liked the smell of rubbing alcohol, and Dr. Hoffmaster's clothes and office always had that wonderful smell.

The second main reason is related to my father. I respected my father who, I thought, until I graduated from high school and went to college at Texas Tech, was the smartest man I had ever known. I did not like him very much but somewhere down deep I knew he

1

loved me and wanted what was best for my life. I think he knew me better than I knew myself. Going off to college I had no clue as to what I wanted to do. Each time I would come up with a suggestion, my father always found something wrong with it. Finally, in the middle of my second year of college, I remember telling him, "Dad, I'm thinking about turning pre-med and going to medical school." This time he did not try to talk me out of it. So truth be known, I became a doctor because my father did not talk me out of it.

After medical school, I did my internship at Harvard's famous teaching hospital, Massachusetts General Hospital in Boston. It is a tradition at the hospital to have a "change" party to mark the transition from the end of your internship to the beginning of your residency. A mark that says you are not quite as dangerous to the community at large as you were just 12 months prior. At the change party, besides the drinking and dancing, awards were given to each of the interns as they were judged by their next in line or junior assistant house officers, JARs, as we called them. I remember how dead-on right those guys were when it came to nailing the character of my cohorts. I was laughing my head off until I received my award, *The Rock of Gibraltar* Award, accompanied by a suitably homemade plaque and a moderate size stone probably dug up between the two wings of the Bullfinch building. It read: "This award is given to the intern who maintains his steadfastness in the face of all the facts."

Like all good humor, there was an undercurrent of poignant truth beneath the ribbing. The somber reflection on this jestful award led me to yet another one of my epiphanies. Namely, others saw me as pigheaded and opinionated and even defensive. I so wanted to be right that I was willing to blind myself to all the evidence around me to the contrary to preserve the importance of my own little melodrama, and I did not even have a clue as to how others viewed me. In my little self-centered world, I really didn't care. I was that prideful.

The lesson learned: We can get so caught up in our own little melodrama we cannot "see" what is really going on. *Our will to be right* in our judgments leaves us unteachable.

When I went into private practice, that was one plaque that did not get hung on the waiting room wall. Instead, it was placed right on my desk so I could see it every day as a reminder to laugh at myself if I found that I was taking myself too seriously.

Chad and the Desire to Be Right

Now listen to Chad during a recent visit to my clinic. He said, as he handed me a hundred-dollar bill, "Doc, I want to pay for an hour of your time. I am 39 years old and falling apart. I hurt all over. I've had to work hard all my life. Nobody has given me anything. I have headaches and my neck is killing me because of a whiplash injury when I was 10 years old. My stomach is killing me. I don't sleep, never have. My lower back is ruined. I have several discs out of place from lifting so hard at work." The list went on.

An hour and a half later when Chad had finished with his story, I had learned that Chad was deeply unhappy with how life had treated him, including a father who had beat him, plus a wife and teenage daughter who did not appreciate him or how hard he worked to provide for them. He was also unhappy with the government's handling of the economy and the general moral decline of the American family.

"Doc, don't you agree that the medical care system is broken? My wife developed breast cancer a few years ago. We didn't have any insurance and it almost broke me to pay for her surgery and chemotherapy."

Casual questioning had revealed that Chad was drinking 6-8 ounces of brandy at night to ease the pain of living and help him try to forget the rotten hand life had dealt him. Obviously, Chad had paid me $100 to agree that he was right. He wanted me to say that he was justified in his barely concealed anger.

What came next is what I want you to think about.

In my encounter with Chad, I had come to the proverbial "Y in the road." However, my choices were four different paths:

#1. I could stop right there and say, "Chad, I believe you need more help than I can offer," and choose not to get further involved.

#2. I could choose to identify with one or all of his physical complaints and order, in addition to baseline lab tests, an MRI of his head, neck and lower back, plus an upper GI series and God knows what else as I reinforce his belief in the pain and suffering his body is experiencing. Trust me, this is the route taken thousands of times each day in doctors' offices and emergency rooms across this country, particularly if you have Blue Cross 38000 in the great state of Texas.

#3. I could have taken one of the most common routes in dealing with this very common office encounter. I could have interrupted Chad's diatribe and concluded his symptoms were largely due to "depression" and started him on one of the several SSRIs available now in inexpensive generic forms and pushed ahead with my busy day and too-full schedule. In my heart of hearts, I would know that I was not really helping Chad with his dilemma. I was simply medicalizing his unhappiness and offering him a 50/50 chance of some temporary relief in his discomfort, knowing full well that the issues in all likelihood would have to be revisited as I pushed him further and further into a medical system that is increasingly adept at labeling things and finding things that are not working as it speeds farther and farther away from the truth of why they are not working. It would be very easy, depending on Chad's lifestyle and genetic predisposition, to convert him into a chronic medical casualty with common, identifiable, labeled medical conditions such as high blood pressure, coronary heart disease, diabetes, depression, and one or two malignancies thrown in for good measure. The only thing protecting him from that fate at this time was Chad's lack of health insurance. Money or the lack thereof was paradoxically holding Chad from a descent into the world of medical madness that millions are living today.

#4. Or....... after a thorough, unrevealing physical exam, I could risk it and go for the gold. I mean "cut to the chase" and really try to help him see his own predicament (i.e., to see himself in his own melodrama). Believing every encounter has the potential to be holy, I go for the truth, unadorned.

"Chad, your judgment on all the events going on in your life has put your body on the defensive, and in so doing, you are attacking yourself. Your dis-ease is the direct result of your wanting to be right about your view of the world as a dangerous, unforgiving and fearful place. Chad, it is possible to see things differently. You can learn this way of seeing, but it won't be easy, nor will it be quick, at least not usually."

"How, Doc?" The defensiveness rose in his voice.

"Chad, you can learn to have a forgiving heart."

"My heart is right with God." Chad interrupted me before the words were out of my mouth.

"You sure could have fooled me," I replied.

"How so?" Chad retorted.

5

"Chad, you have talked to me for over an hour and have not smiled one time. It's pretty clear that your idea of having a heart right with God and my idea of a forgiving heart are not the same thing. Chad, the anger and resentment that I hear in your voice is like taking a poison and expecting the other person to die. It's like you are holding a cleaver over someone else's head when in fact you are holding it over your own. It is impossible to attack an individual or the world without attacking yourself. It starts out mentally, but, ultimately, it has real physical consequences for your body."

By now, I am feeling like the preacher when he asked a farmer what he thought about the sermon the preacher had just delivered. The farmer replied, "My daddy taught me you need to feed the cow, just don't give her the whole bale at one time."

Too much truth all at once is too frightening to many, and they will close up their ears and tune you out. Or panic. Or both.

Joe, I thought to myself, some sow, some reap. Just be satisfied with planting the seed. I have learned that the cure can take awhile, usually quite awhile.

Now for the confession: In my thirty-odd years of practicing medicine, I have had occasion to encounter Chad's problem many times, and it is no exaggeration to say, thousands of times. Truly, the form may have been different, the presenting complaint may have been different, but the battle each of those blessed souls was fighting was the same.

In dealing with this recurrent problem, I admit that I have taken every one of the options listed above. I prostituted myself in all choices except the last one to the god of rationalization. I covered over my own cardinal sins of greed, sloth and anger with the much more acceptable face of "I am too busy." "She really may have something. You know crazy people still get sick." "I'm not trained to handle this." Etc, etc. The plain uncomfortable truth is I stood to profit in some way, financially, psychologically, or intellectually from those people's fears. All I had to do was buy into their own melodrama and choose to let the wonderfully rapid and deft defense mechanism of rationalization clean my hands and wash my guilty mind of any sense of conflict of interest in dealing with, or rather choosing not to deal with, the real battle we were fighting and choosing not to recognize.

You have read the choices. What would you do in similar circumstances? Perhaps before you give your "final answer," we need to ask the question: What is the great battle?

Chapter 2

The Great Battle

Be kind to everyone you meet, as each is fighting a great battle.
Philo of Alexandria, an early church father

No one can serve two masters; for either he will hate the one and love the other, or he will hold to one and despise the other. You cannot serve God and mammon.
Matthew 6:24

Allow the dead to bury their own dead; but as for you, go and proclaim everywhere the kingdom of God.
Luke 9:60

"Battle, you say. Doc, I know all about battles. I'm battling with my wife. I'm battling with my kids. I'm battling with my ex-wife about my kids. I'm battling with my parents. I'm battling with my superintendent. I'm battling with the IRS. I'm battling with my insurance company and the hospital administrators. I'm battling with the credit card company and mortgage company. I'm battling with my weight, cholesterol and blood pressure. I'm battling with cancer, alcohol and smoking. Doc, I'm an expert in battling. In fact my life seems like one great battle." I would agree. I agree that most of us think that all there is to life is battling with something. Almost invariably, we see the battle as something

9

outside ourselves, separate from who we are. If they gave Ph.D.s in battle, most of us would have graduated summa cum laude from the school of life experiences. When I remind my patients that practice does not always make perfect, they look at me in bemused puzzlement. They usually give Ph.D.s to people who have demonstrated some mastery over a subject. Continuing to view life as a battle will not speed up your graduation. Practice just deepens the ruts.

I agree that war rules on this planet and it is awfully easy to get caught up in the battles. I also believe that is exactly where you will be stuck if you don't face the reality that these skirmishes are not the ***BATTLE*** I am talking about.

I do not know for each of you individually when the battle began, but I do know when it started for the collective us. It started when Eve, then Adam, took a bite out of the apple in the Garden of Eden. There has been trouble ever since. As an aside, I want to say that this Garden story, which, while not literally true, is true literally. Taking a bite of the apple, as the devil said, would make us think we were our own gods. It would insure that we would feel guilty because it was not the truth. Somewhere deep down inside each of us, we still know the truth but the awareness of that truth must be awakened. The truth to what? The truth to the following three questions:

> **Who am I?**
> **What am I doing here?**
> **What am I supposed to do?**

The Great Battle I am talking about is the battle in each of our minds as we try to answer these three questions. All the other battling will not be answered until you have answered these three correctly. And there are correct answers. The truth is not relative here. Your very freedom is at stake.

I remember the first time I asked myself these questions. I was actually asking for the answers outside myself. It was my senior year in high school and they were the topic of an English paper I had written in Mrs. Harwell's English class. She had allowed us to write about anything we wanted to and these three questions were my topic. As I recall, it was the only A+ I received in her class, and at the bottom of the page she wrote: "Great questions, Joe, I'm sorry I don't have the answers."

Like so many of us, I pushed those questions out of my mind, but several years later, as a senior in medical school, I began to revisit them. What I came to believe was that there was a battle for what I believed was real. Did I believe the world I encountered with my five senses (sight, smell, hearing, touch and taste) was real, or was there something that transcended the world delivered by those same senses?

I think Christ came to answer that for us for all time. I think in some ways it is similar, but with totally different implications, to the man whose wife caught him in bed with another woman. "Honey," he said, "are you going to believe what I tell you or what you see?"

Jesus told his listeners yesterday and tells us today, " Believe what I tell you and then you will be able to 'see' the truth." The truth comes to each of us as we view this world in which we live and, though perceptually flawed, we still ask ourselves about the things and events around us.

Expressions of the Battle

Einstein said, "There are no miracles or everything is a miracle." That is actually one way of defining the battle. There are many other ways of expressing it. Here are a few:

Nothing is holy. Everything is holy.

I am alone and separate in the universe or I am not alone and separate in the universe.

I am ruled by love or I am a prisoner of fear.

I live in heaven or I live in hell.

I am host to God or I am a slave to my ego or the devil.

I am spirit or I am my body.

I am free or I am a slave.

I was created or I created myself.

I am my brother's keeper or I am not my brother's keeper.

I am myself or I am my Self.

I live in time or I live in eternity.

Nothing matters or it all matters.

I choose sanity or I choose insanity.

I choose to give up all my fears or I continue to fear.

I see the world as one or I see the world as chaotic.

I am safe or I am unsafe.

I choose life or I choose death.

My mind is at peace or my mind is not at peace.

I choose to have or I choose to be.

If you have read this far, I just bet you can add to the list. Look the list over, stop and think about it. Depending upon your culture, age, education, religious training or experience, and, yes, even your genetics, you will decide which of these symbols best describe the battle for you right now. But make no mistake about it, this is the battle or dilemma that you have been fighting for as long as you remember and even longer than you can remember. This is not just a skirmish, although there are many of those. This is the battle that you came to Planet Earth to resolve.

Although he is not just yet ready to concede, it is the battle that Chad, whom we met in the last chapter, came to resolve as well. And from its resolution flows all healing, first of the mind and, more often than not, actual physical healing of your body.

Some of us are more given to introspection than others. I think we can agree on that. Talking with and listening to the living and the "dead" through books convinces me most people have had contact with the transcendent at some point in their lives. I call it a lifting of the veil. The veil that stands between our physical eyesight and the presence of the Holy. Whatever else it may do, it uniformly leaves us with the sense that things, that is, the things we actually look upon or experience through our five senses, may not be just what they seem to be at first or even second glance.

In other words, there is a reality beyond the one to which we commonly ascribe reality. One, I believe, is really real. Whew! These, too, have been called epiphanies.

Let me add here, if you have never experienced such a moment, do not despair. You may have had such a moment but have chosen to forget it or you soon will have one. You can actually prepare yourself for it. Later on in the book, I will give you some practical tips on how to ready yourself to receive it.

Let me tell you about the first epiphany I remember. Growing up in south Texas, in the small town of Edinburg, I had been a slightly above average student. The above average part was probably due to the fact that it was expected of me by both my parents. I did just well enough in school to keep my parents off my case. That was until one day in early November 1963, in Mr. Fernandez's chemistry class.

Looking back, perhaps the extraordinary thing I am about to describe is how absolutely ordinary the day and the circumstances were. It was right after lunch, a time when I should have been sleepy, and we were discussing Boyle's law. For the nonchemist, Boyle's law has to do with the behavior of gases when exposed to changes in temperature and pressure. Not very exciting stuff to most of you, I bet.

Suddenly, I felt myself taken up into, for lack of a better word, a place or other reality. I was surrounded by beauty and order and a sense of wonder unlike any experience that I had ever encountered before. Quite frankly, it was better than sex. It was way past pleasure. I cannot recall how long it lasted, but during those moments I was more than observing. I was lost in the observed. Then it was over. I was still sitting in chemistry class of the second floor of Edinburg High School. Although that experience happened some forty-six years ago, the experience left its mark. It was at that moment I celebrate when I truly became a student. I fell in love with learning, which, as it turns out, is a two-edged sword, ultimately leading to my *Rock of Gibraltar* award nine years later at Harvard's famous teaching hospital, Massachusetts General Hospital.

All that I know was at that time, I loved the "wow" of the experience and I wanted more of it. Thus began my vain and futile efforts in the pursuit of knowledge, as a god. I mistook the setting (science class) for the experience.

Do not get me wrong; there is nothing wrong or right with the pursuit of knowledge but it can be misleading or a delaying tactic. I refer here to pursuing it as a god or idol. Sometimes it can increase the thickness of the veil between this world and the "real" world. You have, I am sure, encountered individuals in your life who knew everything but understood nothing.

By 1973, after nine years of the cramming of science, I came perilously close to being such a "know it all" in my chosen field of medicine. The pursuit of knowledge and all those facts habituated me to seeing the world a certain way. Unconsciously, I was developing a worldview. And without planning it, I was becoming a judge of what was good or bad in the picture I was seeing. Like most of us, I was caught up in my own little melodrama. I had become a slave to my ego. But I had not completely forgotten that initial contact with that "other reality."

Thus, the battle you have come to Planet Earth to resolve is the battle within your own mind of how you will choose to see the world. Your worldview and your role in your worldview. In plain and simple terms.....Who am I?.......What am I doing here?........ What am I supposed to do? This is what I meant by the term introspection. At the beginning of this chapter, we listed several different ways of symbolizing or expressing this battle. Ultimately, they are just several different ways of posing the same contrast. Let's look at a few.

"I am myself or I am my Self." Most of the time we see the

world as a great big scary place, just waiting for the other shoe to drop. In this world, we see ourselves as small and helpless and threatened. That certainly is the way I behaved for a large part of my life. But on a certain day in a small town in an ordinary classroom for a little while, I experienced my "little self" disappear into a very much "bigger Self" that included everybody else's "little self."

"I am safe or I am unsafe." Just think about how differently you might behave if you really felt safe all the time under all circumstances. Just think of the practical implications of this one thought. What do you suppose you would do differently if you really believed and then behaved as if you were not just temporarily safe? "I got a bigger gun and I am a better shot." Instead, your safety did not depend on your defensiveness but instead on who you really are and was a result of who created you and to whom you belong.

"I choose sanity or I choose insanity." Odd as it may seem, sanity is actually a choice. It flows from your worldview. It is the result of the pursuit of truth no matter what the temporary inconveniences that pursuit might cause.

The definition of insanity I like best is doing the same thing over and over and expecting a different outcome. I have written this book to help you make a decision that there is a better way. One that works. Most people who are chronically ill continue to repeat the same ways of thinking.

The definition of sanity that appeals to me most and seems to work for some of my patients is: If I feel uncomfortable, if I am at dis- ease, I am free to choose to think differently or see this situation differently. In other words, there might be a better way of looking at this.

Nickie, Everybody's Keeper

Together, you and I are going to look at these worldviews in more detail in the following chapters. But first I would like you to meet Nickie. We are going to look at this ordinary situation to see how this battle in your mind can have very real and very common consequences you might not have considered, just as it did for Nickie.

Nickie was a forty-seven-year-old school teacher and mother of two grown children. She had been divorced but had since remarried when we first met in my office. She was self-referred, coming to me with high blood pressure and elevated cholesterol. She also had a few pounds she wanted to lose and knew that I had an interest in diet and exercise. Nickie was reluctant to start on the medication that her previous physician had recommended, so she thought she would give me a shot.

On first encounter, I noted she was cute, well-groomed, had a quick and easy smile and certainly showed no signs of chronic unhappiness like Chad, whom we met earlier. On reviewing her social situation, I learned that both of her parents were elderly and her father's health had begun to deteriorate rather rapidly. Her youngest child, a son, was having some difficulties figuring out what he was going to do with his life. And like most mothers, Nickie was worried.

In my review of her faith background, Nickie told me she was a card-carrying Baptist, and though she was comfortable in this latter discussion, I could sense her unspoken question: "What does that have to do with my high blood pressure, elevated cholesterol and weight?" You might feel the same way.

How many times do you imagine this happens in doctors' offices across America every day? It is estimated that sixty-six million Americans have high blood pressure using a threshold criteria of systolic blood pressure > 140mm Hg. Or diastolic blood pressure >90 mm Hg. That's a lot of people and potentially a lot of doctors' visits.

In Nickie's and my patient-doctor relationship, I had come to a crossroad. Here was an extremely common problem. What were my options for her?

Since it had been confirmed that Nickie's blood pressure had consistently been above 160/100 for several weeks according to both her home readings as well as those by the school nurse where she worked, option one, that I do nothing, was not consistent with current medical practice.

Her cholesterol was 256 total with an LDL of 142. Nickie was a non-smoker. Her family history was negative for premature coronary heart disease. She was 20 pounds above her ideal weight for age and height.

What to do about the cholesterol and weight in the light of her high blood pressure?

Option two in our treatment plan could include some combination of diet, exercise and medication. Nickie had a "good" health insurance plan through her school, so the cost of medication was not a top concern. What do you think gets done most often today in routine primary care? Algorithms are available on the computer to direct choices in just such instances for the puzzled physician. Option two is hands-down the most frequent choice for the vast majority of practicing primary care physicians. In fact, computer algorithms can be constructed to perform these tasks quite easily. In the paperless electronic office, I can just see the doctor or doctor's designee entering the "facts" about Nickie's issues and some form of "Big Blue" crunching the numbers and spitting out a treatment plan.

I confess, for far too many years of my medical career, I chose some iteration of option two. It gave me pleasure to think of the neatness of it. Just look at the data and come up with a nice, controlled, logical plan. In truth, I felt rather smug because I have always placed particular emphasis on diet and exercise as first lines of therapy in the treatment of high blood pressure and/or elevated cholesterol as opposed to starting medications right off the bat.

There is an option three. The problem with this option is that it resists digitization. You can not program it into a computer or maybe you can. It involves looking deeper into Nickie's issues; it involves looking deeper into Nickie's life.

To pursue option three, you have to realize that elevated blood pressure and elevated cholesterol are very often simple reflections of a person's level of fear. In common parlance they are pretty good proxy measurements of stress.

In the early 1960s, studies were performed on accountants' cholesterol levels and were found to peak, surprise, surprise, on April 15th of each year. Cholesterol is the backbone molecule for cortisol, a major hormone produced in the body in response to stress. Under the circumstances, elevated cholesterol is just a marker for the body's compensation to a stressful or fear-producing situation. In the accountants' case, that was not being able to get all the work done by a certain time.

"White coat" hypertension, that is, blood pressure that is elevated _only_ in a doctor's office, is an obvious example of fear and its effect on blood pressure.

We had ruled out "white coat" hypertension in Nickie's case, but had we ruled out chronic fear as the cause in our superficial evaluation of her problem? I didn't think so. I decided to look deeper.

"Nickie, do you have much stress in your life?"

"Do I ever!" Relief jumped to her face at the thought that she was going to get a chance to unload.

What followed was a recounting of Nickie's melodrama which involved common themes of dissatisfaction at work, not enough money, responsibility for the care of elderly parents, and what to do with a wayward son whose current trajectory in life was not turning out quite like Nickie had imagined at his birth twenty-three years earlier.

Thirty minutes later, she concluded with, "I bet you think I'm crazy carrying on like this. You didn't know you were going to be a shrink when you came to work today, did you?"

Nickie hadn't realized it at the time but she intuitively had discovered the source of her elevated blood pressure, elevated cholesterol, and her overeating problem. She also discovered what needed fixing. Her mind. The other things were just symptoms measured on a scale of a much deeper problem.

Functionally, Nickie behaved as if she were a little self in an unsafe world in which she had chosen the insane role of the fixer. Fear and its many guises drove Nickie's behavior. She had chosen to be the one in charge of her own little melodrama. She had chosen the right to herself and forgotten the much bigger picture. Nickie freely admitted that all the worry that she had expended in her school classroom, in caring for her parents and deciding what she thought was best for her son had accomplished nothing. In fact, it probably made things worse for her. She admitted she held the insane idea that it was her duty to worry as a teacher, parent and child. She felt guilty if she didn't worry. Though a professing Christian who could easily cite Jesus's instructions to us not to worry, she was behaving as if she were a special case. He must not have thought of her particular problem when he addressed the topic of worry in his time-transcending advice on the subject some two thousand years ago.

What Jesus said was _very_ clear and to the point. He left no doubt about it. He was not subtle and falsely giving you sympathy. He said, " DON'T DO IT!!"

I had decided to go beyond what the computer algorithms recommended, the seemingly easier way that I had chosen so many other times before. I could at this point add some new options on how to approach Nickie's problems.

First, I could satisfy myself that just listening to her woes was therapeutic enough, and, indeed, at the end of the visit, rechecking her blood pressure revealed a 15 point drop in the diastolic reading.

Another option would be to send her for traditional psychological counseling or to a psychiatrist. There are simply not enough of these professionals to go around. The already over-burdened medical system cannot absorb these costs. Nor should it.

My next option is the one that I suggested to Nickie. It is the one I am going to suggest to you. Nickie's worry about all the different outward things in her life - her job, parents, child - were simply reflections of her own deep fears of who she was and who she belonged to. In her case, Nickie had forgotten what she believed. It is what this book is ultimately all about. It is the one sane answer to the battle or dilemma that we came to Planet Earth to resolve. It is the answer or cure, if you will, for the vast majority of medical illnesses that I have seen in thirty odd years of practice. It is the one answer that depends on nobody other than yourself. It is the most cost-efficient of all medical therapies. It is the one that can be programed with much consistent effort to be your response to any sense of dis-ease you feel in your body. Ready????????

FORGIVE AND BE HAPPY

Nickie had three common medical problems: high blood pressure, elevated cholesterol and excess body weight. Odds are you have at least one of these issues yourself. I am saying the emotion of fear has a large role to play in Nickie's medical issues as well as yours.

I am also telling you as I told Nickie that the regular practice of forgiveness is the only mentally healthy way to rid yourself of your fears. I am not asking you to agree with me right now but it is certainly my intent to prove this idea as we go forward. I believe there is a biological basis for why you and I should be forgiving and we are going to look at that next.

Chapter 3

Jesus Versus Darwin

For the good that I will to do, I do not do; but the evil I will not to do, that I practice. Oh wretched man that I am.

Paul in his letter to the Romans. Chapter 7:19, 24.

All the world's a stage and all the men and women merely players.

William Shakespeare

We are going to address some very specific parts of your brain and the emotion of fear in the next chapter, but, first, I think we need to know what each of us is up against in terms of our own potential for "bad behavior." Yours and my bad behavior, not the other guy's. You may believe you know why you do what you do, but odds are you are wrong. That error is related to the timing of the development of the different parts of your brain.

Jesus and Darwin

There is a strident debate concerning the theory of evolution and the theory that our Earth was created some 6800 years ago in 7 days, man being made on the last working day, the 6th. That is according to the account in Genesis, Chapter 1. Man makes his appearance sometime after the first week according to the re-edited account found in Chapter 2. Seems there were revisionists even back then in the days when Genesis was first written or spoken. Just like we do today, I suspect that the tellers of the story updated their information as new things came to light.

If you insist on the literal truth of every word of the Bible, you are going to have trouble with the next few chapters and may want to skip ahead. I could not be a Gideon because I would not swear to the assertion that every word in the Bible was literal. These minor errors should not remove it from your must-read list. It is not called the Good Book for nothing. There is nothing that Jesus taught as recorded in the Bible that is not compatible with man's evolution from lower life forms. Jesus calls the body flesh and he was very clear that he did not worship the human body. "Pluck out your eye; cut off your hand." He made it abundantly clear that we should not depend on this frail thing as our only reality.

Back to School

My second year pre-med course at Texas Tech was called comparative anatomy. (All medical students have to have this course before they are granted admission.) The bulk of the course revolves around the study of various animal species including the shark, cat, pig and monkey. Dr. Rylander did a wonderful job of showing us the links and similarities between the different species, particularly the anatomy of the nervous system. You can literally see the gradual building of an increasingly complex neural wonder.

It was as if you and I rose to the top of the food chain by adding parts to those species of animals below us. It was not that the shark brain did not work for the shark, but it was a matter of necessity if the shark was going to try his fins on land, he was going to need more parts. And, if the shark was going to tell a tale, he would require a lot more parts.

As far as I know, when Mr. or Mrs. Shark gets ready to attack its prey (like you or me), it bares its teeth. The facial muscles pull the skin back on his ugly face to better expose those teeth to do what they were designed to do, eat you and me if we happen to be around when he is hungry. Truth is, we cannot say that the shark is hungry or angry since his communication skills are somewhat limited to "shark talk."

Now, I want you to go to a mirror and look at your face and pretend you are very angry. Don't laugh. Please try this. More often than not, you will find yourself staring at an only slightly modified version of what the shark looks like when he is going to have dinner. Your own cheeks are pulled back, exposing your incisors to better get at your prey. A Big Mac, for instance.

In real life, when you get really angry, particularly if you are a male, you are going to make this expression, and then you are going to feel the emotion of anger. As far as we can know, the shark does not feel guilty about showing his teeth and eating you or me. That emotion apparently was a slow one to develop. Probably about 500,000,000 (five hundred million) years. That is about how long the shark has been around. Fossil studies confirm that the "Jaws" character you see today is pretty much the same as that of a half-billion years ago. It is also how long it has taken to add some more parts to our own very distant relative's brain. Those parts of your brain and my brain are called the frontal lobes. This seems to be where consciousness lies.

The point of this is that our brains share some very primitive structures with other members of the animal kingdom. Amazingly, when you study the nervous system of a human fetus you get a time lapse picture of the evolution of this impressive system. Early in its nine-month gestation, the fetal nervous system will quickly pass through the shark brain stage repeating what it took nature 500,000,000 years to do. This required just a few moments in your mother's womb. As Mr. Einstein said, "It is either all a miracle or there are no miracles." Now, I do not know about you, but this (the development of the human fetus) certainly qualifies on my list as a miraculous phenomenon.

The body that you inhabit developed over a period of nine months, and in that nine months, an outside observer could have seen what had taken nature well over a billion years to accomplish. The body of the Homo sapiens species has been around for only a short time when you compare it to the shark's body. The evolutionary sequence appears to be shark>mammal>primate>hominid ancestor>Homo sapiens.

Your outward behavior today has many determinants that appeared very early in the evolutionary chain. Looking back on the history of man reveals what we are capable of doing when push comes to shove, no pun intended.

Type A Behavior and the Shark

Let me give you a very concrete example in today's world where we can see this ancient shark biology push its way into everyday human behavior. It is found in the artificial classification of behavior called Type A.

I met Myer Friedman in 1973. Dr. Friedman was a physician with an absolutely charming character, whom I credit with stimulating my thinking when it came to heart disease. At the time, I had interrupted my training at Mass General and taken a position as a project officer in the Cardiology Division at the National

Institute of Health (NIH) in Bethesda, Maryland. This was just at the end of the Vietnam War and I had been offered the position as an alternative to taking my chances with the Army draft. I thought it would give me a chance to see if academic medicine was a good fit for my personality and leapt at the offer when it came. For me it was a no- brainer, almost a shark "no-brainer."

It was considered a two-year fellowship in cardiology, even though I had no formal patient contact during working hours.

I think these two years did more to "save my life" than any other years since. It was a period of intense learning for me as I worked my way through Mortimer J. Adler's *Great Books of Western Civilization*. It also gave me time to catch up on my medical journal reading, having largely put it aside during my hectic internship work schedule of 110-120 hours per week.

I began to develop a philosophy of life and medicine during those two years. It allowed me to put into context all the "facts" that I had acquired thus far and integrate them with the clinical experiences of that first year of medical internship. I was glad for the respite.

That is where Myer Friedman comes into the story. Part of the job of our division was to review applications to the NIH for research grant money in the area of heart disease. Grant applications came in from all over the United States, including some of the most prestigious names in medical exploration. It afforded me a panoramic view of what was considered cutting-edge cardiac research of the time, the early seventies.

Most of the work, my physician colleagues and I agreed, was not very exciting. It was more or less boilerplate work. There were some notable novel exceptions, including the development and use of the intra-aortic balloon pump to tide the heart attack victim over until their own heart recouped some of its pumping power. This device is still widely used in the intensive care unit today.

This device received tons of research money when it was developed.

At that time, Dr. Friedman was seeking support for his research into the link between personality type and coronary disease. He and his partner, Dr. Ray Rosenman, had just published a book called *Type A Behavior and Your Heart.* It had been a publishing success, but the research behind it had not drawn the financial support of the academic community that Dr. Friedman needed. So he applied to the Heart and Lung Institute for funding.

I had a special interest in the origin of this thing we call a heart attack. My interest was in the minority of victims (approximately 10%) who had a very peculiar finding. That finding was that though patients had experienced a classical heart attack with chest pain, death of heart muscle, EKG changes, and elevated cardiac enzymes, their coronary arteries were completely normal. The arteries were wide open at autopsy and wide open when catheterized after the event. The more common ruptured fatty plaque and subsequent clot were not to be found.

What was going on? It appears that spasm of the blood vessel can account for some, but not all, of these interesting "outside the box" cases. It was Dr. Friedman's contention that a chronic pattern of behavior could explain most of the heart attacks we see in clinical medicine. He called this Type A behavior.

It was characterized by a number of noted traits, chief among them a sense of time urgency and free-floating hostility. These patients were often agitated and slightly to overtly angry. One of the physical characteristic observations in interviewing these patients was and is a subconscious tic of baring their teeth when they are talking to you. They are not aware of it, but are very hard-pressed to suppress it even after it has been repeatedly pointed out to them.

This, my friend, is that very old shark face coming through in their behavior. It is an ancient sign of the "attack mode" that we all carry inside our heritage. This behavior, like heart attacks before age sixty, is much more common in the male of the species. It is present in females to a much lesser degree. Interestingly, as women have entered the competitive business world, we are seeing more heart attacks and more grimacing.

Dr. Friedman freely admitted to me that he himself exhibited Type A behavior and thought it might have a genetic basis. He felt a bit helpless in dealing with it in himself and thought benzodiazepines (Valium) should be given to all people who suffer from it. He told me that Valium in this case was like insulin to a diabetic. Despite knowing its origin, the late Dr. Friedman treated himself with bypass surgery a few years later as he was unable to come up with a cure to his own insight.

The Heart and Lung Institute turned down his request for support, at least in the early years. They were still interested in things that were easier to measure, things that sounded more "scientific" like the intra-aortic balloon pump. Human behavior has too many variables to allow it to be analyzed and put into a computer. The thought that certain chronic patterns of poor thinking could lead to heart disease was considered too superstitious at the time.

I believe Dr. Friedman was correct in the direction he was looking as an explanation for a very common event. I think he was describing the far end of a spectrum of what anger and attack thoughts can do to you. I think it plays a far bigger role in the everyday development of inflamed and clogged arteries that continues today.

I think it is a good example of some very ancient behaviors driven by very primitive reflexes, well below your conscious awareness. I believe it shows what you and I are up against when we talk of the flesh and its drives and once again proves that "some things that can be measured don't count while other things that can't be measured do."

Thus far, I have maintained that most of suffering, perhaps all of suffering, comes from our individual desire to be right, that is, our desire to be right about our ability to judge as good and bad the events of our ordinary lives. Thus, every Tom, Dick, Harry, Mary, Chad, Nickie, Eileen and Joe has found himself or herself right square in the middle of Pandora's box started by the metaphorical Eve and Adam a long time ago. Did I create myself or was I created? There seem to be two natures at war in you and me. One is biological. The question is, "Am I capable of being more than my biology?"

I further maintain that conflicting worldviews are the inevitable consequence of just such a desire to be right and that this conflict gives rise to the majority of medical illnesses we as humans suffer. At least, the same medical illnesses I have tried to treat in this small town of East Texas over the span of the last thirty years.

Finally, it is my belief that there is only one practical way out or mental solution to this mind-splitting dilemma and that is to learn to forgive and be happy.

In the spirit of transparency, let me be very specific about this term forgiveness as I have used it thus far and will maintain throughout the book. My encounter with Chad and many others like him have convinced me of the rather obvious fact: We do not always see eye to eye. Thus the need for defining our terms.

Forgive: *to give up resentment against or the desire to punish; stop being angry with; to give up all claim to punish or exact penalty for an offense.*

Webster's Dictionary

First, let's look at a vivid yet simple case of the successful application of this principle before we delve into the fascinating neurobiological basis for its necessity.

The Brawl

Kirk came to see me at the suggestion of his mother. He had been ill for several months prior to his seeing me. He had complaints of nausea, vomiting and weight loss, all of which were interfering with his work as an investment advisor with a major brokerage house.

He was thirty years old, bright and ambitious by his own admission, but was not doing well as he had lost thirty-five pounds over the last two and a half months. His primary care physician had suggested an upper GI, as well as lab work to try to better define what was going on.

I confess this would have been my recommendation for twenty-five of my first thirty years of practice. My reflex behavior would have been to repeat what I had done so many times before.

In light of what you have read so far, you might guess what course I took. I decided that since he did not, at that moment, appear in any immediate (the next day or so) danger of dying, that I would find out more about Kirk's life around the time his symptoms started. I stopped, I listened, and I heard. Something you must learn to do. Don't be so quick to do what initially you think is right.

It seems that Kirk had taken a trip to see his father with whom he had strained relations for several years. This compromised relationship began with the divorce of his parents when Kirk was in his early teens or perhaps earlier. This is a particularly vulnerable time in a young man's life and emotional wounds are common.

Kirk, who himself had been divorced after two years of marriage, had taken his then new girlfriend along on the visit to his father who lived several states away. While there, he and his father had words. One thing led to another and his dad had physically thrown Kirk out of the house, with a few punches thrown in for good measure. Kirk had felt betrayed and left the house and his father in anger. He had not spoken with his dad since.

"Doc, you have to agree that was a pretty lousy thing to do to your son, don't you?" he asked, as the sense of indignation burned in his eyes.

"Yes, Kirk, but you, not your father, are in my office complaining of insomnia, nausea and vomiting and weight loss. Kirk, you seem to be a bright young man. Are you very introspective?" I asked. "Don't you think it is at least interesting that your symptoms began shortly after the melee?"

"What are you getting at? Do you think this is all in my head, that I'm doing this to myself?" Kirk asked incredulously.

I shrugged my shoulders as I allowed the truth to dawn on him. I have found that self-discovery sticks better when you are led to it on your own. Don't be in a hurry. His reflex answer, as you will see, may not be the right answer. You have to allow others time to think.

The light began to reappear in Kirk's initially indignant eyes and his nose, which he literally held up as if something stunk, dropped to its more normal position on his otherwise quite handsome face.

"Do you mean that my getting mad at my father could make me not sleep, make my stomach hurt and not be able to keep my food down?"

"Yes, that's exactly what I am suggesting, Kirk. You could have gotten an ulcer or gastritis from that episode."

"And what am I supposed to do now, how am I supposed to get better?" Kirk pleaded. "Do you think I need some medicine to settle my stomach, maybe something for my nerves?!" he added.

"I think you know the answer," I replied. Although Kirk did not like the answer that he came up with himself, it did not keep him from recognizing the truth of it. The truth of what he should do next.

"I guess you are telling me I've got to forgive him. That sucks. He gets off scot-free for what he did to me."

"Kirk, you haven't talked to your dad in two and a half months. How do you know he has gotten off scot-free? He might be in his doctor's office right now complaining of chest pain for all you know." Like Chad, I told Kirk, "You have to make a choice. You can be happy and healthy or you can be right.

"Actually, it just comes down to biology. How you think ultimately affects your biology. The smartest man in the world taught us that, two thousand years ago, and your reluctance to accept the truth doesn't change the truth. Truth is truth no matter how much you believe it sucks."

If you are presenting your offering at the altar, and there remember that your brother has something against you, leave your offering, and go your way; first be reconciled to your brother, and then come and present your offering.

Matthew 5:32

Before Kirk left that day, we scheduled an upper GI series for one week hence; I wanted to see how effective our visit had been before we launched an expensive, and most likely unfruitful, battery of tests. It turns out I did not have to wait long.

An incoming call from an unfamiliar area code greeted me forty-eight hours later. It was Kirk calling from work. "Doctor Davis, as much as I hate to admit it, I am better. Though I haven't called my father yet, I went home and in my mind forgave him." Sheepishly, Kirk added, "It dawned on me, something I said might

33

have provoked the whole big mess."

Now Kirk was a baby on his spiritual walk. His mother was an ordained minister but Kirk was in that skeptical phase of his life, and he was not altogether sure of my methods. But he was broke and had no insurance and this seemed like a no-risk bet. So he took it.

I told Kirk, as I am telling you, you must first forgive before you are granted understanding. It does not work the other way. The only person's thinking that you have any chance of control over is your own. The happy news is that you can learn to control these attack thoughts. In fact, your sanity depends on it. That is, your sanity depends upon thinking correctly. And thinking correctly is healing. Since the mind directs the body, the body will usually follow along.

Within a week, Kirk was literally transformed into a smiling, healthy-appearing, non-vomiting person. It took a few days, but when I saw him again, I could tell Kirk was on the mend. We cancelled the X-ray and blood work, realizing we could reschedule them if necessary in the future if Kirk did not continue to get better.

I confess there have been many times in my career when I have taken the seemingly easy way out of just such an encounter, blinded by the obvious as I focused on the symptoms feeding my fears of missing something "real." The ulcer, the gastritis.

Several months later, in fact, while I was writing this book, Kirk, being inquisitive, asked me, "What do you mean by the biological basis for forgiveness? Doc, I thought that forgiveness was all religious, spiritual stuff."

Here was my answer. Kirk "got it." I hope you will too.

Why Did I Do What I Just Did?

If a young child accidentally breaks a glass or spills some milk, you usually forgive him or her pretty quickly. Why? He did not do it on purpose. Even if he is a willful child and appeared to do it on purpose, when asked why he did it, his response of "I don't know" may hold more truth than you might think.

The law is much more lenient with crimes of passion - those that involve extremes of emotion, such as anger or its exaggeration, rage, than those that involve preplanning, premeditation, if you will. The temporary insanity plea is used by defendants successfully because we as a society believe a sane person can lose touch with reality and become insane temporarily and quite literally not know what he is doing. His actions or behavior appear to be driven by forces that never reach his own personal level of consciousness or awareness. We as a society forgive him because he was not in his "right mind."

Now, let us go from the extreme to the ordinary. You and I, as a general rule, take responsibility for our actions or behavior as we go through our ordinary lives because we believe we are in control of our actions. We, in fact, are aware or conscious of what we are doing. Consciousness is a feature of animal life. Self-awareness is an attribute that separates man from his lower cousins on the evolutionary chain. We believe that we are aware, that we are conscious.

Or are we??????

The Grand Experiment

Most great discoveries in science are quite simple and seemingly fortuitous. Scientists were looking for one thing, then found something quite different. The discovery of X-rays and penicillin are just two of many examples that can be cited.

In the fields of neurobiology and neuropsychology, the

experiment of Dr. Benjamin Libet, at the University of California at San Francisco, is just such a seminal simple experiment. Dr. Libet was looking at the timing of the appearance of brain activity, the chicken or the egg sequence. He hooked volunteers to an electroencephalography machine (an electrical device for recording brain waves) to look at brain activity during the process of making simple decisions such as when to move a finger. He showed that the process which leads to an act starts about three-tenths of a second before an individual is consciously aware of it. In other words, even in volitional acts, you are, in fact, an observer, not a decider. Your awareness is always of the past. You are self-aware but only of the past. The present could thus be defined as a state of being unaware of the past or future, that is, just being aware.

I believe this explains the feeling that you and I have experienced at one time or another of having deliberately done something we had not actually wanted or intended to do. I think this explains the Apostle Paul's lament in Romans 7:15 & 24 when he says, *"For that which I am doing, I do not understand; for I am not practicing what I would like to do, but I am doing the very thing I hate." "Wretched man that I am."* He felt trapped by the drives of his flesh. That is why he felt so wretched. His passions or emotions were working themselves out in his thoughts and behavior, just like what happens to you and me and Dr. Friedman. He knew he was powerless on his own to control them all the time. Some of the time, maybe, but not consistently. This is what we are up against and just like Paul, we need supernatural help to gain control. Valium may temper the fires, but it will not fix the problem, and Jesus knew it. Shakespeare said we are all actors on a stage. Looks like he was right.

If all the world is a stage and we are but actors on it, would it not be more peaceful if you and I cut the other actors some slack? More directly, would you not be happier if you carried this thought in your head all the while you went about your ordinary life interacting with all the other deluded actors who still believe they know what they are doing?

Cutting the other guy some slack or forgiveness just makes good common sense because, after all, he is not all that different from you. He is fighting the same battle and he is just as lost on the battlefield (or stage) as you and I are.

To repeat, it is very important to note here the sequence of events in any given conflict. You must forgive first, then you will be given understanding. It is an extremely common error to reverse this sequence (i.e., to seek to understand first before you forgive). Kirk had done that with his father. His desire to be "right" had clouded his understanding of the situation and his role in the fight, and it was not until he forgave his father that he was able to see it with a higher perspective. He realized that, truth be told, they both needed to be cut some slack. By the same rule that you judge, you will unconsciously judge yourself. Jesus also said that two thousand years ago. Pretty accurate insight into your and my psyches?

Kirk's example is that of a subacute illness resulting from the harboring of resentful and angry emotions. Those same emotions triggered biological responses in Kirk's body, which, if left unresolved, eventually would have led to a neat and tidy disease such as peptic ulcer, ulcerative colitis, mucous colitis, et cetera.

Kirk's case is not a rare event. It happens all the time in doctors' offices everywhere.

We as physicians like our illnesses neat and tidy. That is why we like to name them; it gives us a sense of control; it gives a sense of orderliness to our job and our restricted worldview. We see a sick person and we try to fit him into one of our learned labels. Psychiatrists have developed a very long list of nameable mental disorders called the DSM (Diagnostic and Statistical Manual of Mental Disorders). It gives the doctor and usually the patient a sense of security to have those bothersome symptoms named. That is why we call biology, sociology, anthropology, and medicine, descriptive sciences as opposed to the instructional sciences of math, physics and chemistry. Over the years, *I confess* I derived mental pleasure in putting my patients in a named box. It stroked my ego to figure it out.

"Gee, doctor, I am so glad you found what's wrong with me. For a while, I thought I was losing my mind. I even thought I was doing this to myself." Often you are, dear brother, often you are.

If none of us truly knows what we are doing when we are doing it, but instead are aware of what we have done after we have done it, what is it that causes us to do what we have done? The answer may surprise you. Fear is the driving force behind the vast majority of human behavior both now and down through the ages ever since Adam and Eve took that first bite in the Garden.

Let us take a closer look at this primal driving force that I believe is responsible for so much illness, death and destruction.

Chapter 4

The Biology of Fear

All the world is a narrow bridge over which people need to cross. And the most important thing, the most crucial thing is to not be afraid.

Reb Nachman, founder of the Hasidic sect of Judaism

Work out your salvation with fear and trembling.

Philippians 2:12

It is silly to go on pretending that under the skin we are all brothers. The truth is more likely we are all cannibals, assassins, traitors, liars, hypocrites, and poltroons.

Henry Miller, American writer

He did not give us a spirit of fear but of power and a strong mind.

II Timothy 1:7

I do not know if you took biology in high school. Biology, which is a descriptive science, is broken down into botany and zoology. For our purposes we are restricting ourselves to zoology. I am encouraging you to become interested in the biology of your body for a while. I am doing this because in order for you to make a decision about who you are, you need to understand the

39

implications of your answer to that question. If you decide you are your body only, then your behavior will be best understood as the workings of a very clever beast. Henry Miller, whom I quoted above, is pretty close to being dead-on right as to what to expect in a world where the players think they are separate bodies going about their separate business. A world that is restricted to the "biological" worldview.

If you want to be happy and healthy, then you are going to have to learn the signs your body will give you to let you know it is receiving signals to fight or run. You have to learn your thinking ultimately controls much of the "fight or flight system." The subject of the biology of fear is simply too important to skip if you are ill and want to be well and happy.

In this chapter we will discuss your brain in more detail. At the back of the book, I will give you some very readable and fascinating references so you can look into this subject in more depth.

The gist of the chapter is that each of our bodies has a very hard-wired fear response designed to protect it from getting eaten before it has had time to get copies of its DNA into the merry-go-round of evolution.

It is this biological fear response that has made us the cannibals, assassins, traitors, liars, hypocrites and cowards that have dominated human history. Fortunately, this does not have to be your fate nor mine. We can choose differently.

In the previous chapters we have learned our desire to be right about our individual worldview has led to a battle within our minds for which is the truth. Are we each alone, self-created, unsafe, and at the mercy of a seemingly cruel, or at the very least, indifferent jester, just a forgettable cosmic accident? Or are we safe, secure, free, limitless, loved, parts of a harmonious eternal whole? Have we been created by a loving Father who really does have our best interests at heart? If you choose to believe the first opinion, then your behavior will, for the most part, be driven by fear. If you choose as your identity your physical body, then fear follows unavoidably. That is how it is made. That is its biology.

It is my further contention that the mental act of forgiveness is a necessary, learnable skill to be applied in all circumstances that involve conflict, no matter what the other person <u>appears</u> to choose to do. That is, if you desire to be happy, sane, and physically healthy. You have to learn to think if you are to avoid being controlled by your emotions. Fear is the failsafe reflex and driving force of most of your day-to-day actions unless you learn to stop, listen, hear, forgive and then speak. Your own thinking is the only thing you can have control over. Otherwise, you will simply react to the lower driving forces.

Why forgive? Remember, the other guy is just as lost and fearful as you are because of how the brain works. The biological basis for fear is fascinating, but, before I launch into that discussion, let me define the term "fear."

Fear: *A feeling of anxiety and agitation caused by the presence or nearness of danger, evil, pain, threat, etc., timidity; dread; terror; fright; apprehension.*

Webster's Dictionary

Biological Basis of Fear
Back to School

Let us review some facts. In the last chapter, you have seen that the body you are occupying right now as you read these pages does not appear to have been created overnight. I am not saying that it could not have been. I am saying I have not seen it happen personally. I have also told you the formation of any infant animal

41

species in its mother's womb is a pretty amazing piece of work. I stand in awe of all the complexity of the various parts coming together over such a relatively short period of time. In your and my case, nine months. I can certainly see where the intelligent design theory has its appeal.

In the previous chapter, I focused on the development of the human brain as part of the entire nervous system. This is an artificial division I am using to make a point.

The fact is that your and my nervous system developed in our mother's womb at the same time all the rest of this thing we call our body was developing. There is great danger in looking at something in isolation. It does two things. First, it gives the false impression we have figured out this thing (in this case the nervous system) or, given enough time and resources, we will in the future figure it out. The second danger is we easily lose sight of the forest for the trees. Scientists frequently fall into this trap. There is a joke about scientists that says they know more and more about less and less until they know everything about nothing. You can laugh, but this goes on every day in labs all across the world. Not all scientists fall into this trap, but many do.

With that caveat in mind, let us look a little closer at your brain and my brain in a metaphorical sense.

As the human brain developed over the last whatever period of time, it automatically became more complex. Your brain is certainly more complex than our monkey cousins, and the monkey's brain is more complex than the shark's.

The brain has been compared to a computer. I have a problem with that as a whole, but for lack of a better analogy, I am going to borrow it for a moment. If you call up Dell and tell them you want them to build you a computer, they are going to start out with the basics and then add on parts, programs or hardware depending on the complexity you need or for how many functions you are going to use on that computer. At the core of the personal computer, you have the hard drive. You can add whatever else you want, even make it dance an electronic jig, but you are still going to have to have a hard drive to channel the power through or it just will not work.

I am simplifying here but believe this simplification works for our purposes. Consider the shark's brain as your hard drive and the rest of your brain as add-ons. You did not get to call Dell and have your brain built to your specs. You are stuck with the one you have.

As our distant relatives climbed out of the sea and started walking around on dry ground, they eventually started to gather into groups and develop a social structure. This involved more complex interactions so more parts were added. They did not get rid of the hard drive, the shark brain. They added fancier structures, including something called the limbic system and some gray matter right behind your forehead called the frontal lobes. Now do not ask me who <u>they</u> were. I do not know. I do know, however, if you examine the behavior of some our closest primate brothers, the chimpanzees and the bonobos, you can see a lot of similarities to some of our behavior. With a lot of training, you can get the chimpanzee to behave about as well as a two-year-old child, which is to say not too well. Monkeys do have frontal lobes; they are just not as big or as wrinkled as yours and mine. But most of the deeper structures in the monkey brain look very similar and appear to have similar function to those deeper structures of our brains.

Remember Dr. Libet's experiment from the last chapter. Your "outward behavior" appears to be driven by some deeper structures below your consciousness or awareness. Above, I noted you can train a monkey to do certain things by giving him or her certain cues or rewards like a bite of a banana. The monkey will repeat the behavior over time, given the same cues. We call the giving of this reward a reinforcement. It means we can pretty much predict what our friend the monkey is going to do because we have selected what behavior we want and have reinforced it. What we, in fact, have done is elicit a certain behavior by activating the reward center in the monkey's brain. This reward center is also known as the pleasure center. It has a very definite location in the monkey's brain that can be mapped out. You and I have similar areas in our brains. When you eat a piece of cherry pie or drink a (real) Coke, you stimulate this pleasure/reward center. It is also a behavior that is largely done without thinking at all. Your feeding behavior is the result of the workings of your deep shark brain. I believe that is why eating disorders are so notoriously difficult to treat. It is a behavior that has evolved over at least five hundred million years. Now that is a behavior that is hard to change!

Now if the pleasure/reward center was the only center in our brains, oh what a merry Christmas we would have. Unfortunately, there is a dark side to this anatomy lesson. The Grinch did indeed steal Christmas by giving you and me and our happy monkey friends a fear and punishment center that I want to hone in on here. We will revisit the pleasure center later. The pleasure center and the fear/punishment centers are a part of a complex system called the limbic system.

Limbic System or Emotional Brain

The areas of the brain which include structures called the amygdala, hippocampus and hypothalamus are collectively called the limbic system. Their development in the human body occurs well before the portions of the brain from which you derive your consciousness or awareness and have everything to do with sex, anger and eating. So it would come as no surprise that it is also called your emotional or motivational portion of your brain. It is the border area between your conscious brain and your shark brain.

I am not trying to make you a neuroscientist, but these structures are so important to understanding why you do what you do, you cannot ignore them. These "lower" or more primitive structures drive more of your behavior and thoughts than do the "higher" or more recent frontal lobes of your brain.

To start this dialogue, let me confess that I have been afraid most of my life, at least that part extending back to early childhood. Psychological studies of children confirm the almost universal presence of fear in children. Our recall of the specific fears depends upon the timing of the threat and the development of our central nervous system, particularly, those parts of the brain involved in the formation of our retrievable memories.

Interestingly, some fears appear to be more common than others. But each of us as individuals have, on the basis of our culture, parental upbringing, life experiences, and yes, even our genetic heritage, by adulthood developed our own unique set of fears.

The fear response is triggered by a whole set of symbols, which may include words, colors, shapes, tastes, scents, postures, noises, textures, or any combination thereof. Most often, the fear response is a direct result of the input of our five senses and is processed temporally before we are aware of it. I bet there are things you are afraid of that you have not told anybody else. Most of us are too ashamed to admit them. Each of us has our own demons.

Neuroscientists would say the fear response takes place subcortically, or below your consciousness or awareness (an attribute of your evolutionary newer, wrinkled, gray frontal cortex of your brain).

Interestingly, newborn infants have what is called a "startle reflex," brought on by loud noises or the physical stimulation of moving a limb or the body in which there is a general electrical discharge of the central nervous system. It involves a reproducible picture of arms and hands thrown back, extension of the neck, and a grimace on the face which is usually followed by the outpouring of hormones including epinephrine, norepinephrine and cortisol.

As an adult, you would see this same startle response if you were suddenly surprised by a gun-toting robber. Your hands fly up, you extend your neck and very commonly grimace. This happens quite quickly, before you have time to process your next move. This fright response is the adult variant of the startle response seen in the newborn.

This outward show of fear is accompanied by internal activation of the "fight or flight" response. From the perspective of the individual human body, this has served its purpose very well.

Fight or Flight System

When you are frightened, a number of chemical changes occur in your body. The subsequent rise in insulin levels, the elevation of the blood pressure and heart rate, the reflex increase in general muscle tone, the outpouring of glucose by the liver all transform you into a defensive, possibly fighting, machine. And if not fighting, quickly fleeing the scene.

You can well imagine that if you were being chased by a saber-tooth tiger or a stronger, bigger, fellow human being, this would be a good system to have in place. All mammalian species have it, and you as a member of the animal kingdom are a mammal. At least your body is.

The Kluver-Bucy Syndrome

To illustrate how important these lower or more primitive structures of the brain are, let me describe an experiment that has been repeated often by neuroscientists in the study of the mammalian brain. These studies are usually performed on monkeys because what scientists want to know is what drives human behavior, and the assumption is that if these same experiments were performed on humans, they would behave similarly.

If you remove part of the limbic system that lies inside the temporal lobes of the brain, it causes changes in behavior called the Kluver-Bucy syndrome. This is, as comedian Steve Martin might say, one "wild and crazy" monkey. First, it is not afraid of anything, I mean nothing. Second, it is curious about everything but forgets rapidly. I suspect that is why it remains so curious because it cannot remember anything about its environment, so it remains childlike in its investigation of its surroundings. Does this sound familiar to you? Early on, the limbic system is not fully developed in a one to two-year-old. In many ways, the toddler behaves fearlessly.

The animal behaves very orally and has a tendency to put everything into its mouth, sometimes trying to eat solid objects. Mothers, does this sound familiar to you as you have watched your babies' behavior? They seem to want to stick anything they can get a hold of in their mouth. That is the shark brain coming through. It is part of a primitive feeding reflex.

Finally, it has a sex drive so strong that it attempts to copulate (have sex) with immature animals, animals of the same sex, or even animals of a different species.

These experiments are done on mature animals. During early teenage years, masturbation is a normal developmental phenomenon. This is also part of that shark's brain coming through without the fully developed limbic area to moderate it. There are recorded cases of bilateral destruction of part or all of both amygdala in human beings. Guess what? These people behave very similar to that monkey.

The next step in understanding what makes you, me and Sammy

run comes from other extremely fascinating - and I might add reproducible - studies involving electrical stimulation of different parts of this limbic system. Most of the studies have been done in non-human primates as well as other mammalian species. You can occasionally get away with stimulating the brain of patients while performing surgery on the brain for other reasons. Studies conducted during these procedures do confirm in general what we learned from the animal experiments. But you better have them tied down well as you will see below.

Fear and Punishment Reactions

If you stimulate certain areas of the hypothalamus, a very important part of the limbic system, an animal shows certain signs we associate with fear and punishment. It cowers, hunches down, raises its arm as if to ward off a blow, its pupils dilate, and, occasionally, it will defecate or urinate.

Have you ever been so frightened that you wet your pants or lost control of your bowels? If so, these are the result of activity of those same centers in your brain.

Stimulating other areas of the hypothalamus occasions that same defensive posturing, but it will also elicit something more. Fear morphs into hissing, raising of the tail, spitting, growling, and if provoked in the least, savage attack. Scientists call this rage. You probably call it "losing your cool".

I admit I have experienced rage two times in my adult life. They were memorable events because of how nearly lethal they were.

In both cases, after the fact, I felt physically ill, totally depleted. In both cases fear morphed into anger which spread like a wildfire resulting in the sensation of rage. In both cases, which occurred fifteen years apart, I remember vividly observing my speech and tone of voice as if it were someone else in control of what I was doing as I stood helplessly by. Those more primitive parts of my brain were in control.

The next morning I quickly called, apologized and asked for forgiveness because I had seen what the retention of the emotion fear/anger can do.

Note the sequence.....fear > anger >rage >think >forgive. This is just the opposite from what I am telling you that you must do if you want to be happy and healthy.

Kirk and his father, whom you met in Chapter 3, probably had a heck of a discharge of their limbic systems when they were duking it out.

What I think is more important for our discussion is the sequence of behaviors and how stereotypical they are. The first sign of the fear response is piloerection. The hair on the monkey's or dog's or cat's back will stand up just like it does on you when you are particularly frightened.

The defense posture and signs of fear precede the anger and rage response. This is why you will hear me say that "anger is just a mask for fear."

These fear responses are accompanied by a huge outpouring of hormones such as epinephrine and cortisol with a striking elevation of blood pressure and heart rate. The immune system is now put on high alert. I am glad I didn't have a blood pressure cuff available when I "lost it". This is where strokes and heart attacks do occur. We will come back to the effects of a heightened immune system later when considering autoimmune diseases.

Attack Thoughts and Fear

I am discussing the biology of fear to put you on notice of what you are up against. These are very primal heavily reinforced behaviors. You have lots of attack thoughts every day. They have their origin in your fears and your defense against those fears. They do not usually produce rage but they do have a low-level effect on your body's chemistry.

Stripped of the extremely thin veneer of civilization that we humans operate in, you are going to be faced with some, at least initially, repelling thoughts.

Each of you in your natural state is a fearful, fighting, eating, drinking, sex machine. This is behavior controlled only by the flesh or your biology. The emotion fear can unleash the shark's brain and it can take over.

Obviously, most of us do not go around pouncing on our next door neighbor, and, we have moderately good control of our sexual appetites. Although the incidence of obesity is certainly rising, the majority still manage to push away from the table before they pop.

You have your frontal lobes to thank for that - at least for the large part. This part of the brain which lies just behind your forehead was the last feature to be added evolutionarily and is the last part of a child's brain to mature on the path to adulthood.

You might say it is what keeps those primitive impulses in check. Again, at least for the most part, it allows you to do the harder thing. I like to think of them, that is the frontal lobes, as responsible for our ability to live in cities of ten million with a police force of only several thousand.

This is where the manipulation of the fear response steps into our picture. You, by your own thinking, can cover up or inhibit your fear response. You can even deny its presence. Psychologically, we call these defense mechanisms.

Unwittingly, your fear response is frequently manipulated by others. This is just another way that the strong prey on the weak in your perceptual world. Unfortunately, some of this preying is done by people in a position of trust, who ought to, yet do not seem to know better. For the purpose of this book, I am alluding to the medical profession, and I do not exclude myself from this observation. Thus, the title of the book. Remember these are the confessions of a repentant medical whore.

I admitted earlier that for most of my life I have been afraid, and as much as I would like to take your fears from you, I cannot. You have to give them up yourself. You have to fight your own demons and it is not easy. As you face, them you will have fear and trembling, literally, but the payoff is worth it. Your happiness, your health, your real life and, most important, your freedom await you. For most of my medical career I prostituted myself to the service of fear. Though I did not recognize it at the time, fear is the devil's or the ego's calling card.

Let me give you a concrete example early in 1978 to illustrate how subtle and innocent and, you may think, even desirable the manipulation of another's fears may be.

Larry and the Pizza Dinner

I met Larry, a married, childless, 37-year-old man a few months after opening my practice. He had high blood pressure, an elevated serum cholesterol of over 300, and was a committed three-to four pack-a-day smoker. He also had a positive family history of premature coronary disease, his father having died in his early 40's of a sudden cardiac death. He had, as I recall, a "nervous temperament," which, according to his wife, resulted in Larry's becoming angry quite easily, sometimes at the drop of a hat. Larry exhibited what Myer Freidman called, in his seminal book on personality types and heart disease, Type A behavior. What I am now saying is Larry was afraid and neither he nor I knew it. His anger was a mask for his fears.

Armed with my recently completed internal medicine training and my preventive medicine bias, I felt rather smug when I told Larry he was a disaster waiting to happen. Note, at the time, I did not bother to ask Larry what he was afraid of. I was too happy that he seemed to fit into one of my own little algorithms and I took not just a little pride in my recognition of his predicament. I gave him a copy of a low-fat diet, told him he must start exercising and immediately stop smoking if he wanted to avoid big problems down the road. I left his management of his stress to chance, recognizing even then that opening his Pandora's box would probably involve looking into my own. And I was too young and confident in myself and my knowledge to do that back then.

As you might imagine, Larry followed none of my recommendations as he guiltily admitted in our follow-up visits. In fact, my advice probably just added to his bag of fears as he awaited the fulfillment of my warnings.

Less than two years after that first encounter in my office and subsequent routine follow-up visits, Larry and I met again, this time in the local emergency room of our hospital. Now Larry was no longer asymptomatic. When I entered the ER, Larry was clutching his chest, sweating profusely, and covered with the semi-digested pepperoni pizza he had partaken of less than thirty minutes before his heart attack symptoms started. Nausea and vomiting are sometimes prominent symptoms of a heart attack. So is the urge to have a bowel movement. These are just exaggeration of the "flight or fight" fear mechanism.

"You gotta help me, this pain in my chest is killing me," were the first words out of his vomit-encrusted mouth.

Dutifully and with a moderate amount of pleasure, I did just that. I did it with pleasure, not because I liked seeing Larry hurt but that this picture was so neat and tidy and predictable. It fit so perfectly into my little algorithm of what to do in the case of a myocardial infarction. I went about treating him using the current medical standards of the day, which, in retrospect, was not all that much. Oxygen by nasal cannula, lidocaine by IV drip, and hefty doses of morphine for pain relief - that was about it. This was in the days before we had cardiologists, cath labs or clot-busting drugs in every small town.

After writing admission orders to the ICU, which covered the first few days of his anticipated two-week hospital stay, I began to rehearse in my mind the speech I was going to give Larry when his pain settled down and his mind cleared somewhat from the mind-mucking effects of the pain medication.

Larry and I were going to have a "come to Jesus" meeting. There was only one small problem; I had left Jesus out of the equation entirely.

Early the next morning, I marched into Larry's room like a medical drill sergeant. After the initial pleasantries and a cursory physical exam that confirmed Larry was indeed stable and at the moment pain-free, I got right to the point.

"Larry, you know I've been telling you, you have to stop smoking; now I mean it."

"Yes, sir," Larry meekly replied. "I quit as of yesterday, not another one."

"Larry, where is pepperoni pizza on that low-fat diet I gave you months ago?" I queried.

"I know, I know, but I couldn't help myself," he guiltily, but quite honestly, replied as he ducked his head like a whipped puppy.

"One last thing, Larry, the nurses are going to start getting you up in a chair today which I hope will be the new start of a regular exercise program that I want you on after you leave this hospital. Otherwise, you are going to be right back in here the next time, that is, if you are lucky enough to survive," I concluded with a forceful flourish.

And then, that was it. I left the room, never really putting myself in Larry's shoes, content that I had done my duty as a physician to catch Larry in a vulnerable state while I laid down the law trying to bend those frontal lobes of his to my way of thinking, using fear as the motivation.

Guess what? It didn't work then and it hasn't worked since. Within six weeks, Larry, now free of pain, was back to his old ways of smoking and eating whatever he wanted to, and when the thought of programmed exercise came to him, he rested until it passed.

I had simply reinforced his and my ideas that this was a scary world, he was his body, and the next shoe could drop at any moment. And although there was some truth behind my proclamations, I had left Larry without a Guide to help him with his great battle, and, coincidently, help me with mine.

Chapter 5

The Guide

*Therefore I say to you, any sin and blasphemy shall be forgiven
men, but blasphemy against the Spirit shall not be forgiven.*
                                                    Matthew 12: 31

Truth is marching on, nothing can stop it.
                                    Emile Zola, French novelist

Nothing good is engineered of the flesh.
                                    Xystus I, 7th Bishop of Rome

*Even so oxen, lions, and horses, if they had hands wherewith to
grave images, would fashion gods after their own shapes and give
them bodies like their own.*
                                    Xenophon of Calophon 475 BC.

Now the gloves are off. We are going to look at the truth squarely
in the face. Even though it may seem "to suck" as Kirk put it, it is
still the truth. Truth, in fact, is not relative. There is a truth which
is true no matter that you and I may have trouble acknowledging it
or seeing it. It remains the unchanging truth. Even if you were to
give me a second *Rock of Gibraltar* award, I will not budge from
this belief in an unchanging truth.

Two thousand years ago, Jesus Christ climbed upon a cross, was crucified and buried. And, as the single most important event recorded in history, three days later He arose from the dead. The battle is over!!! He overcame this flesh and proved that we are more than this body; we are spirit. The problem is that unless you surrender to and identify with the One who won the battle, you still believe there is a battle to be fought. And, trust me, you will fight that illusory battle in your mind and behavior, as though in a very bad dream, as you seek and do not find. On your own, by your own devices, the war will rage.

Secular humanism would say that man, by his own efforts or collective efforts, can ultimately perfect himself because at his core, fleshly core, he is good. I believe that you can improve a character trait or two but as long as you believe you are your body and identify with it, you will suffer the consequences. You may even win a few "skirmishes" by individually behaving in a moral manner. But God help you if worldwide food and water become in short supply. At that point, most of you will react with the biological response of fear.

But when you accept the Atonement, His death and resurrection, you are sent this wonderful Guide (the paraclete or Holy Spirit) whose function is to awaken you from this very bad dream. He will reveal to you that the struggle to know who you are is over. You are Spirit and you are His. If you would have told me I would have written these last two paragraphs when I graduated from medical school in 1972, I would have told you, you have lost your mind. I was armed with all the scientific facts that I could cram into the brain, but the supernatural was not anywhere on my radar screen. Oh, I had heard the term Holy Spirit, but it had as much meaning to me as some absurd Greek word signifying gobbledygook. I did not relate to the term, it did not relate to anything in my practical experience or education. My experience of the holy was confined to the experience in high school that I described in Chapter One. My only practical experience with the holy I had found in science, particularly theoretical physics and organic chemistry, not practical physics or laboratory organic chemistry, but theoretical. The holiness to me was in the orderliness of the subject. I allowed myself to play in mental la-la land, as I recognize in retrospect, because the neat and tidy world of my thoughts was more orderly than the practical world of laboratory physics and chemistry. Things looked more sublime when I considered them in pure thought rather than the mess of a bench full of beakers and physical contraptions. Playing in la-la land of aesthetic beauty gave me temporary peace of mind. It was pleasurable and thus reinforced itself. However, the peace of mind did not last. I had not yet awakened to the presence of the Guide; I was not ready yet to receive it as the gift that it is. I had more illusions of control to be rid of first.

My own experiences make me very understanding of my physician brothers who place such great emphasis upon the observable, the measurable. It gave me, as it gives them, a sense of control of their worldview, their own melodrama. It keeps the fears at bay. Psychiatrists know this defense mechanism as intellectualization; you and I use it a lot in our everyday lives. Doctors just get paid better for it. Thus it is psychologically heavily reinforced; more money, more pleasure temporarily, more repetition of the behavior.

My first real wake-up call to the inadequacy of my godless worldview came the first few weeks of my medical internship. The very sick patients I was seeing in the emergency room and the wards rarely fit my tidy preconception, my neat structured algorithms I had placed my hopes on in my quest to "cure the world."

Instead, I was faced with this messy thing called medical care made up of human suffering from chronic maladies whose origins appeared to be so distant as to be hardly recognizable. Even then, it dawned on me that quite often, their suffering was a result of what they were doing or had done to themselves. Occasionally, I saw a neat and tidy "fascinoma" that was like a drink of cool water in the parched wasteland of, to my eye, incurable, chronic conditions of diabetes, strokes, arthritis, cancer, dementia, obesity and the final physical ravages of chronic alcoholism.

I remember my first experience with fear morphing into panic as if it were yesterday. Sitting with my fellow intern, Don, and our leader, first-year resident Denny, we were discussing the previous night's admissions when it dawned on me that I was in the "box." I was due to be the intern on call that evening for our team. I was scared. First, it was just a sense of unease in my gut, but within a few moments, I was internally beside myself. I could feel my heart racing and I couldn't seem to get enough air. This was July 1972 and the term "panic attack" had not gripped the public's nor most physicians' imagination.

I was afraid I was not going to be able to fill my role in the melodrama of my own life. I was projecting forward all my fears, the most poignant: What if somebody dies and I fail to do my job?

I didn't share my feelings with my colleagues for I was too ashamed. After all, how would this affect my image? I wanted them to see how calm, confident and secure I was in my abilities to handle anything thrown at me. Eventually, I made it through that day and night and many subsequent ones largely by accepting the fact that the worst that could happen on my watch was the patient could indeed die. His heart could stop beating, his breathing cease, and I knew what to do if the worst case scenario did, in fact, occur. I was well trained in the skills of CPR and performed them regularly and competently. Though the panic attack went away, there was that vague sense of dis-ease every second or third night of the on-call rotation. I was not aware of the Guide. I was afraid and I felt alone.

As the year drug by, I self-medicated with alcohol on my nights off, an average of four beers each off night and a 24 case on the rare free weekend. I struggled to ease the pain of living as so many of us do, treating the symptoms, not recognizing the root problem or battle and totally unaware of the very real help available.

Falling back on my love of learning, I sought solace, or at least enlightenment, in delving into the wisdom literature using Mortimer J. Adler's _How to Read a Book_ as my guide. At the back of that book is a wonderful list of the great books of Western civilization. I tackled these, hoping to find something that would help me reshape my worldview into something not quite so scary. I, in fact, was consulting with the great minds of the past to see if they could help me with the picture my five senses were delivering to me. Had they seen the same things I had and what did they make of it?

Included in this search was my first adult experience with the Bible. I used the Cliff Notes version called _The Story Bible_ by Pearl S. Buck. I thought, at least, I would not be at complete loss when talking with the Christian patients I encountered. Since I considered myself to be a nominal Christian, having been raised attending the Methodist church, this would give us common ground for communication.

The Story Bible, which is now out of print, was in paperback form; the Old Testament was covered in a bright red wrapping, the New Testament in a soothing blue. Their brevity did serve one purpose, I read them through and through several times, giving me a broad understanding of what the authors were getting at but nonetheless leaving me just as fearful as when I started.

In the beginning, I did hone in on what Solomon was saying in Ecclesiastes, "It is all vanity and there is nothing new under the sun," and it struck a responsive chord within me. At that particular point, I felt a certain kinship with him despite the passage of some 2500 years. I felt he would have been a good beer-drinking buddy as we both looked out on a futile world or at least a meaningless one.

Since then, I have read the real version of Ecclesiastes many times. It is, in fact, my favorite book in the Old Testament. When I told my mother that a few years ago, she had trouble believing it. She knew me to be happy most of the time and felt, as many do, that the author's conclusions are depressing. To me, they are an exactly correct view of a Jesusless world by a man at the top of the food chain.

If you deny the existence of anything beyond this perceptual world, you are erecting a jail for yourself and one of your own making. Mentally, you are creating a "hell" for yourself if we use the term "hell" as meaning separation from God. Another way to put it is that if you identify yourself with the body as being your reality and the reality of human existence, then this picture will cause you despair. That is, if you dare to think about it. But most people do not really think; they just react.

Chapters 3 and 4 present a fairly accurate picture of the perceptual world of your and my five senses. Most observed behavior in human terms is driven by the emotion of fear but does not actually occur in that sequence. We first have the reflex behavior and then fear follows. You and I experience this emotion we call fear as a sense of anxiety or agitation and we lose our peace of mind. Most of us are reasonably successful at suppressing this sensation because it is uncomfortable and we simply choose not to think about it. Usually, this sense of discomfort is **not** felt in the head but the center of the chest and abdomen and it spreads from there.

Most people lead lives of quiet desperation because they have "seen" the world as accurately as the five senses can deliver it, and it is not a pretty picture. So most decide not to think about it as their subconscious mind mulls it over and delivers up these issues in your dreams. You still have physiologic changes of fear though you are not aware of them.

I believe this is why insomnia is such a growing complaint worldwide, but particularly in America. It is phenomenal the number of people who use sleep aids today. Those include everything from Tylenol, Benadryl and Melatonin to prescription tranquilizers and sleeping pills. One of the biggest abuses of alcohol is for this purpose. The purpose is to numb the mind so you do not have to think. You do not want to be afraid.

The brilliant Irish playwright, George Bernard Shaw, made this observation roughly one hundred years ago. Some think it is humorous; I believe it to be true. He said, "One percent of the people think. Two percent of the people think that they think. Ninety-seven percent of the people would rather die than think."

Mr. Shaw was an atheist and obviously somewhat cynical and, being at the top of the food chain, he could afford to be witty. It was not spoken in compassion but instead from that cancerous position of cynicism.

I agree with Mr. Shaw's observation, but for an entirely different reason. I think most people choose not to think because the world as it is seen without forgiving eyes is simply too sad to bear.

I think that is why Jesus wept outside Lazarus's tomb before He called him out to life again with him. I think He despaired of how few understood who He was and how few would walk through the open jail door of their own imprisoned minds. He knew the biology of our bodies. He knew in our despair we would seek satisfaction where it would not and still cannot be found. He knew we would try everything before we tried Him.

He knew we would seek pleasure using the body as an end in itself. He knew we would trap ourselves in the frail jail of the body, seeking peace of mind through the obsessive pursuit of stimulating that pleasure/reward center of the limbic system we discussed earlier. He knew we would use alcohol, sex, drugs, eating and the pursuit of riches. He knew we would try to avoid despair by using work or multiple relationships, always seeking for just a little more. He knew we would pursue length of years and good health to avoid despair and would put off until tomorrow looking at the truth of the predicament we had imposed on ourselves. He knew that until we gave up, we would be trapped by our own desires since the short pleasure would not ultimately be successful in easing the pain of living because we had mistakenly identified this world as the only kingdom there is.

He knew there was another way of thinking that would give us new sight. He knew that in order to view this world we live in without despair, we would have to see it through His eyes. His forgiving eyes.

I tell anyone who will listen that if they want to be happy and healthy while living in this dog-eat-dog world, you must literally learn to see it with Jesus's forgiving eyes. Numbing your brain to what your eyeballs see will not work.

I confess I have tried all the ways I listed above to numb my senses, to give me peace of mind, and they did not work. They did not work for Solomon, they did not work for me, and they will not work for you.

Dinner or Diner

Thirty-seven years later, I can state a truth I have held for a large number of them and it is this: In this world of form made up of separate bodies and co-populated with a myriad of life forms, you are either *dinner or diner* at any given moment. This is the perceptual world delivered to you by your five senses and moreover to the five senses of your body's very, very distant ancestors, both of the same species and your mammalian cousins. Without supernatural assistance, the frontal lobes of the brain are of precious little help in changing this rather bleak picture.

In this picture, one-cell organisms rule despite the comings and goings of kings, dictators and presidents. The strong prey upon the weak. The hubris of most of our anthropomorphic views is just that, hubris. Without the assistance of another vision given as a gift by a loving Father through His guide, the Holy Spirit, you are stuck in your assessment of yourself as only a biological phenomenon. You are stuck in the flesh.

That which is born of the flesh is flesh, and that which is born of the Spirit is spirit.

John 3:6

Holy Spirit: *In Christianity, comforter, intercessor, teacher or advocate.*

Webster's Dictionary

Sir William Osler, considered the father of modern medicine and still revered today, was wise beyond just the scientific facts of his day at the turn of the last century. In an address to graduating medical students in 1900, he made the assertion that in order to be a good physician, you must have a secular faith in man or a real faith in God. In my early struggle to make sense of the suffering I was seeing as a young practicing doctor, I tried to avoid making a choice in these views and, just as many of you do, I tried to keep a foot on each path simultaneously. I remained lukewarm to both. My uncertainty played out in my practice as I projected my own fears on to the lives of the patients I encountered, just as I described with Larry in the last chapter.

My conviction that most of the illnesses and suffering I encountered were self-induced was leading me toward cynicism concerning man and his ability to help himself by his own good intentions and efforts. I began to see the physical world like Mr. Shaw.

At this point, like a dilettante, I continued to sample various philosophers and their philosophies. They had their points of wisdom just like my friend Solomon, but I always found myself unsatisfied. They did transiently stimulate the reward center of my limbic brain, but they were not enough to give me peace of mind. Although I did not recognize it at the time, I was learning the way this world views learning: *Seek and do not find.*

My Christian Seer

As somebody who went through a Christian conversion experience at age fifty-four, I can tell you firsthand that it was a singular event. Not in a world-shaking sense but in my worldview-shaking sense. Obviously, I am not alone in noting that defining the event may be impossible, but something happened that night that marked a new birth for me. I started over in life. I now know that these sorts of events have been happening for millennia and continue today.

I will only summarize the experience as being one in which something was done to me not by me. It is almost impossible to put the experience into words, for as symbols, they fall woefully short in describing the supernatural. I admit that my curiosity led me to read the famous Dr. William James' book, <u>The Varieties of Religious Experience</u>. Several months later, I was still trying to understand what had happened to me, as my old ways of looking at things became completely reversed. It was as if I were headed in one direction only to find myself taken up, turned around and heading in exactly the opposite way.

I have come to understand that after such an experience, you see everything as a matter of grace. You are so happy to be where you are, you would not want to change a thing about your life out of concern for altering the outcome in some way. The event occurred in October 2002, but without my realizing it, the road had started much earlier.

As I indicated before, I had received my two-year perfect attendance Sunday School pin confirming, that for several years beginning as a young child, Mother insisted that my brother and I attend Sunday School every Sunday we were not sick. Church was another matter. Easter and Christmas were "must" days; otherwise an hour of religious instruction each week would have to do.

At that point, I would not have called myself fertile soil for what was being taught. I did enjoy the Kool-Aid and cookies for as long as they lasted. MYF (Methodist Youth Fellowship) on Sunday evenings and church-sponsored swim parties continued up to age fourteen or so, until the more primal call of **Girls, Girls, Girls** raised its distracting head and I allowed myself to be led off the path. I re-entered the road slowly and skeptically in the later training years and those first few years of private medical practice.

An early turning point was an encounter with my Seer. He was a delightful, mentally sharp, 90-year-old retired Methodist minister I met in Estes Park, Colorado. We used to go trout fishing together. He said something one day that I could not make sense of at the time. One day, traveling to the local lake, he stopped and made this comment: "Joe, don't go to Jesus Christ until you can accept Him intellectually." That was it. That's all I can remember of all our prior and subsequent conversations. He, of course, knew me better than I knew myself and I still treasure his advice today.

Let me add quickly, a belief in the historicity of Jesus Christ does not automatically eliminate fear and wipe out anger, but what that belief did seem to offer was hope of better things to come. Hope was not the certainty I was after, but it certainly trumped despair. Thus began my faltering steps back to my faith in God.

Melanie in Jail

Modern medicine with its reliance on technology, computers, clinical pathways of care, treatment algorithms, and lab measurements is seriously close to losing sight of the forest for the trees. It is also rapidly losing its heart.

A few years ago in an editorial in a prominent medical journal, the author suggested that issues of faith, not being provable by the "scientific" method, warranted a disclaimer release by the medical practitioner if it were to be offered in his or her office. After my initial incredulity at the thought, I laughed and found myself in agreement with the proposition. Prayer and contact with the Guide can radically change lives and deserves a proper warning of its possible side effects.

Melanie, whom I recently saw in my office, illustrates these points nicely. This event also poignantly reveals the failures of our current medical system to meet many patients' needs.

Melanie was a 41-year-old married mother of three who self-referred as she heard I had some skill in getting people off "benzodiazepines," to use her own words. Benzodiazepines include a whole class of tranquilizers including Xanax, Ativan, Klonopin, Valium, and Librium. She heard that it might be dangerous to stop them suddenly and was at a loss as to what to do next. She had made a resolve to get off of them "once and for all." She had heard I approached things differently from mainstream medicine, and with the encouragement of her mother, made the appointment to see me.

As I now do with all my new non-emergency patient encounters, I warn people up front that I am a "born-again Christian," in the truest sense of the word and that I consider Jesus my right-hand Man, and if they feel uncomfortable with that, then perhaps I am not the doctor for them. I do not have them sign a silly piece of paper, trusting that directness leaves no doubt about biases in our relationship. Like the late Scott Peck, M.D., I think a spiritual history should be part of any complete mental or physical evaluation. Not to judge. Simply to find out where the patient is at that moment.

Melanie quickly confirmed she as well as her mother and father were all "born- again Christians" and felt comfortable using the language of religion in our discussions of her problems. Thus began Melanie's fascinating tale of gradual imprisonment.

Melaine described herself as being "high-strung" for at least all of her life she could remember. She was painfully shy in elementary school and improved little during her preteen years. Her first encounter with the medical system began shortly after the birth of her first child some nineteen years ago. At the time, she noted she had "skipped heartbeats", diagnosed as PVCs (premature ventricular contractions) and was prescribed a beta blocker. When that did not work, the tranquilizer Xanax was added.

What followed was a gradual paralysis of her social functioning highlighted by increasing fears concerning nearly everything, to the point her anxiety literally ruled her life. She developed agoraphobia (fear of crowds) and reduced as much as possible all non-essential social interaction.

Interestingly, she continued to perform her duties as a school teacher remarkably well, receiving awards and recognition as a result. The entire time, she admitted, it took increasing doses of anti-anxiety drugs to get her through her day. She consulted psychiatrists and counselors with only temporary relief with their suggested behavioral modification exercises, including yoga and relaxation techniques.

She developed strong guilt feelings over her seeming inability to control her own thoughts. Antidepressants were added to control her obsessions and compulsions, but instead of helping, she blamed them for a significant weight gain that added to her sense of failure.

Her concern over the relatively new problem with her memory and the lack of improvement in her fears brought her to the conclusion she needed to try something different.

"Dr. Davis, if I go back to my family doctor or the psychiatrist, all they will want to do is change my Ativan to some other tranquilizer and my Zoloft to some other SSRI," she said, betraying in her sophisticated speech someone with too much experience in the medical system. "I know there are people in jail today that are more free than I am; there has to be a better way," she added with finality. "I feel like such a hypocrite when I tell my own children and the kids in my class not to use drugs when I have become such a drughead myself. None of my close friends would ever guess what I am doing. It would be so nice if I could get to the point where I don't care what other people think of me. I have been so afraid at times during the night that I have literally peed in my pants."

I told Melanie, and I am telling you, medicine and all its "science" can treat your symptoms but it cannot solve your real problems.

"Melanie, you are trapped in your fears and you won't truly be free until you can answer these three questions: Who am I? Why am I here? What am I supposed to do? I can answer the first two for you. They were guaranteed when you confessed your faith in Christ.

"First, you are not your body, but a spirit child of God, wholly loved forever, not separate from all of life around you but part of the same.

"Second, you are here to wake up to that reality, receive as a gift the peace of mind this awakening bestows and, in turn, in a sense of gratitude, pass it on to all you encounter in the very holy and blessed life you are living.

"The last question I can't answer for you, and, paradoxically, neither can you. That's a mystery that you will discover for yourself as you give up being a slave to your ego or Satan and instead become host to God, who will reveal in your very ordinary life, day by day, moment by moment, His unique plan to use you for His purposes.

"Stop asking Him to take your fears away. You must give them up yourself. It will become easier and easier as you surrender your right to yourself and your own melodrama and put the fruit of the knowledge of good and evil back on the tree, letting Him decide all things for you. That is what the Holy Spirit is for, that is precisely what He does. He is your very real and personal Guide and Comforter as you gradually awaken to those first two answers. And you will discover that fears are, in fact, illusions and an unreal part of a very bad dream.

"I will not pretend that this new road you will travel will be easy, although for some it may. You have been playing your own tapes of your melodrama for far too many years for you not to experience some fear and trembling as you let go of the idols and amulets you have used to avoid or put off the only really important decision you will ever make.

"The past is over because of what Christ did on the cross for all of us two thousand years ago. The future is unknowable because it is the future and you will be surrendering it to the Holy Spirit, thus ensuring it will not be a repeat of the past.

You must become skilled in living in the present moment, which does not come naturally but requires both your vigilance and His supernatural help."

I ended the encounter with a specific plan for the gradual weaning of her tranquilizer as it can indeed have serious physical side effects if stopped too abruptly. I explained the phenomenon of rebound anxiety as the frontal lobes of the brain emerge from their artificial suppression.

I gave Melanie a homework assignment I would highly recommend for you should your fears get the best of you. I asked her to read Matthew 6:25-34 twice daily for thirty days. I asked that it be done first thing in the morning before she got out of bed and the last thing at night before she turned out the light. I told her there is a great mystery in these words and real physical effects on the psyche as well as subsequent effects on blood pressure, heart rate, blood sugar and cortisol levels.

Melanie had some experiences with psychoanalysis that left her fleetingly more comfortable but ultimately unsatisfied. Performed at its best, it can be an act of love, but the problem remains that the patient is left to their own devices to cipher future behavior and therein lies the flaw; that is, the reliance on self or, just as bad, the judgment of the therapist himself to answer the third question: What am I supposed to do?

I have used Melanie's case to illustrate another point. The real work of giving up your fears begins after you confess you need help. You can claim that you have been "born again" as Melanie said, but due to your own mental laziness not progress beyond that confession. It is as if you are saying to Jesus, "Fix me." He has opened the prison door. You must do the hard mental work of walking through the door. The nice thing is from the time of your confession and rebirth, you do not have to walk alone.

Before she left, I made Melanie an appointment for one month, at which time I told her we would begin further teaching in the art of present-moment living, the only place your can experience the Kingdom of God.

Chapter 6
Present Moment Living

Therefore do not worry about tomorrow for tomorrow will worry about its own things. Sufficient for the day is its own trouble.
Matthew 6: 34

Behind the cross is the devil.
Miguel de Cervantes in *Don Quixote*

The present is never our goal: the past and present are our means: the future alone is our goal. Thus we never live but hope to live and always hoping to be happy; it is inevitable that we will never be so.
Blaise Pascal, French philosopher

If you want to be happy and healthy, then you are going to have to give up something. "Dr. Joe, do you mean there is a sacrifice involved?" Yes, I am saying there is one big sacrifice you must make to be truly happy and healthy all the time. Here I am speaking of mental health but the neutral body usually follows like a well-trained lamb if it is now used in the service of the Spirit as a means of communicating to others your own peace of mind.

The sacrifice?

WORRY!!!! Yes, you cannot be consistently happy if you insist on your right to worry. You cannot say to yourself, "I know that worry is a sin but Jesus just didn't understand what it is like living in the twenty-first century with all these complications."

Really? Can you hear your desire to hold on to your own little melodrama here? Do you really believe that worry is expected of you in order to be considered worthy of His love? Could it be that worry is actually pride on your part that confirms what a good parent or wife or husband or employee you are? Could it be that you use worry to set yourself and your family apart from those awful Joneses down the block who let their kids run wild?

Could it be you are using worry as an excuse not to put the apple back on the tree? Could it be you are using your fretting as a way of saying God and His Son are not big enough? They cannot handle my situation, it's too special. Aren't you really saying that you feel down deep you are special? I asked Nickie and Melanie these same questions concerning their worries.

I want you to remember this: Worry and doubt are the devil's calling cards.

You have probably heard the following, but it bears repeating until you truly get it: **Hard work** never hurt anybody, but **worry** will kill you every time. Your fear and worry block your ability to hear the Holy Spirit.

When you worry, it always involves something in the future or guilt over the past. The only place you will find lasting happiness is in the present moment.

When I find myself worrying, it signals me that I am not all here in the **NOW.** You must to be vigilant in this. I know that it is easier for some than others and I believe easier for a man than a woman. Although there are no absolute rules, worry seems to occur more the older and wealthier you become. It seems to be more common the more complicated your life becomes. As Jesus said, the cares of the world and the deceitfulness of riches will choke off His word. His calming words.

I remember very vividly the day I decided to set a new goal of living one day at a time. I was sitting in the sunroom of our home in Boston. It was June 1977 and I had just completed taking my Internal Medicine Board exams and I asked myself: What next??? Like most medical students, I had developed the habit of being very goal-oriented. Again, like most of my fellow students, I had become obsessive- compulsive about reaching those goals. Actually, being obsessive-compulsive about details helped us to be better physicians and/or surgeons.

We used to laugh that if they were to treat obsessive-compulsive disorder indiscriminately, ninety percent of our medical school class would be on medication or in therapy.

I admit, I was an extreme example of this phenomenon, and the awards and honors I received just served to reinforce the behavior.

First had been the goal of getting into medical school, which required me to demonstrate a certain level of proficiency in the sciences which were spelled out in the admission catalogs from the various institutions. That was to get through pre-med.

Next came medical school itself, which was indeed both a physical and mental challenge, particularly amid a group of bright, competitive classmates. In school there were all those goals. It was always the next step. Get through gross anatomy, get through neuroanatomy, get through pathology, get through the basic science years, get through my clinical medicine rotation, get through my junior year. Then it was get in the best internship at the best hospital for my chosen field. For me, this was Mass General in Boston. All that goal-setting cultivated my ambition. Ambition, I have learned, can be a treacherous thing. At least, it was for me. It was nearly always ready, fire, aim as I pursued my own personal melodrama. After all, I had learned that self-actualization was "good" from the psychology course I had taken in my pre-med studies.

All that goal-setting, and frequently their accomplishment, had led me to the *Rock of Gibraltar* award I noted at the beginning of the book; it also led me to miss a lot of what was going on around me. Finally, it led me to believe in the reality and importance of my own little melodrama and the illusion of control of its outcome. It was a very egocentric world which, by the time I was musing in that sunroom, had progressed to the point that although I believed in something vaguely bigger than myself, I saw no irony in the decision to exclude God from my plans to live in the world presently as if His opinion did not really count. I had taken the French philosopher Blaise Pascal's wager. In my youthful prime, I saw no need for a personal God, no need for any help carrying out my plans at that point. I was still ambitious enough and cocky enough that I believed I could do it on my own. Those at the top of the food chain infrequently see any need for higher help. So, like Pascal, I saw no downside risk to the idea that there was a God; I just wasn't interested in His getting too involved in my own personal affairs.

Prayer in my life was confined to saying thank you for the meal with my family at night and asking God to help the less fortunate, with no sense of irony in ignoring any part that I might offer in helping Him to do just that. Although I offered my orison as much as a sense of duty to set an example for my two sons, the regular practice of it, unknowingly, was the first step in a very long journey of accomplishing present-moment living, my stated goal. Grace works like that.

When Melanie, whom you met in the last chapter, returned for her follow-up visit, we began the process of teaching her the beginning steps of present-moment living. It is an art that does not come naturally, but the simpler your life becomes, the easier it will be.

The Story of Ancient Zen Master

In my senior year of medical school, I had read Herman Hesse's <u>Siddhartha</u> which is the story of the life of the Buddha. I think there are some wonderful positive truths to be found in Buddhism, particularly Zen Buddhism. But make no mistake, it is not Christianity. I think you can achieve a "mindless state" by following the precepts of the Buddha, but for me, Buddhism is not active enough. Love is a force, a creative force, and I believe you receive the Holy Spirit as a gift. I could not overcome my desires by following the enlightened path. I personally need the constant real presence 24/7 of the Guide.

Zen Buddhism has some lovely stories that present you with mental paradoxes, and I use the following in my practice frequently. Sometimes looking outside Christianity can actually increase your appreciation for how paradoxical but true some of the sayings of Jesus are. For example: "He who would be master must be servant of all."

There was once a Zen master living in the Far East in a small village. One day the village elders brought a young woman pregnant with child and confronted the Zen master. "This woman says this is your child." "Is that so?" he replied. Taking the child into his home, the master lovingly raised the child since the mother had run off with another man shortly after the child's birth.

Twenty years later, the mother now middle-aged, tormented with guilt, returned to the village. She once again sought out the village elders. They in turn called the Zen master before them saying, "This woman now repents, saying the child is not yours, that she had never seen you before that day twenty years ago. The Zen master replied, "Is that so?"

Like the Zen master, we have to learn to embrace life on its terms rather than our own selfish ones as we venture into God's irresistible future. I want you and Melanie and Nickie to be able to live like that ancient Zen master. Your identification with the most profound and seminal event in recorded history, the death and resurrection of Jesus Christ, I believe, allows you to do just that. Furthermore, I believe the Zen fable can become true for you.

Thirty-two years later, I concede that I have not mastered the art but I am closer.

What follows is the plan I offered Melanie and Nickie and, as I mentioned in Chapter 2, I believe to be good practical tips on how to prepare yourself for some wonderful epiphanies.

#1. Acknowledge your need for help.

As long as you feel reasonably comfortable, you will continue to rely on what has gotten you by so far. The ready availability of a whole host of idols prevents most people from feeling uncomfortable enough to acknowledge they need help. Seek and do not find. Most of the time we simply choose another idol rather than recognize we are lost. I certainly sampled my share of the list before giving up. Here are just some. You may be able to add a few personal ones of your own: tranquilizers, anti-depressants, alcohol, sex (either same or opposite gender), pornography, busyness, work, ambition, food, exercise, anger, laziness, lying, pursuit of knowledge, wealth, smoking, the Bible, religion, collecting, hunting, illicit drugs, parenting, art, fishing, and "good works."

Some of these may surprise you, others not, but any of these things, worldly or not so worldly, if pursued as a means or an end in themselves, stimulate the pleasure center of your limbic system enough to keep you satisfied with your own efforts at controlling your own little melodrama. You are happy enough and do not see a need to change. I like to call this the "practical approach" to life and it remains the biggest obstacle to abundant life. It is not that you want too much, but that you are satisfied with too little.

I had a prominent, successful businessman in my office recently wanting a renewal on his Ativan prescription. He took 1 mg. daily on most days. His answer to my question if he would like to try another way was, "I am happy enough." That is the case with most of us and we see no need to face the battle at a much deeper level. Melanie was miserable enough that she just might stick with the plan.

#2. Simplify your life.

Stating the obvious, the vast majority of us have far too much sensory input into our central nervous system today. The voice of God, your Guide, is very quiet, and especially in the beginning, you need to literally shut out some of this other stimului. Some of Melanie's own thoughts about her personal melodrama are too loud for her to hear her Guide.

There are too many things vying for your attention. Blackberries, cell phones, texting, computers, television, twitters, tweets, e-mails, all are taxing your brain with sensory overload. Although the miracle of manipulation of light to allow this pseudo-connection of the world's population is impressive, I think it may hide a potential danger.

That danger is the worship of the human brain. While the human brain is indeed quite impressive and the evolution of its structure is beautiful, it does not deserve a place on anybody's pedestal. Deprive somebody of sleep for 48-72 hours, and you will be struck by what a tenuous strand it holds on orderly thought. Where did human reasoning go?

Google's desire to put all human knowledge on its servers is hubris of Biblical proportions and its motto, "do no evil," is a mask that bears careful watching. "Illusion reigns" would be my sobriquet if ever asked for a substitute. The human brain is a much overrated organ when listening for your Guide. Your heart, literally, is much more reliable when seeking the Holy Spirit's direction. It will be the spot where you can recognize the presence of fear first, as you become more sensitive to its urging and checking.

Get rid of all unnecessary clutter in your life, and all clutter is unnecessary. Remember, you do not own your things, they own you.

Make a vow that everything you own, house, car, furniture, jewelry, land, stock and bond portfolio, etc., is for sale at any time if the right buyer comes along. Put no limitations or preconceptions on where your Guide may take you.

Pack your bags, travel light, and be ready to go, should be your constant, simple attitude.

Some of the most angry and fearful people I have met are the fussiest, busiest, and most religious. The thought of quietly asking for guidance just for today is totally at odds with their own projections of their melodrama into the future.

#3. Remain teachable

Do not make up your mind beforehand as to what you think your greatest strengths and weaknesses are. In all likelihood, you are wrong. You don't know squat. I didn't know squat about what was best for my life and neither do you. As long as you plan on holding on to your own vested interests or own preconceptions as to what is best for you, you have not surrendered enough.

Each morning when you get out of bed, say to yourself, "I don't know where to go, I don't know what to do, I don't know what to say. Show me the way." You can say these out loud at first. I don't care where you are in your life, work, or education. That is how you should start your day every day from now on.

I have already shown you by the experiments of Dr. Libet that you have not known what you are doing, despite your certain confidence in your own "free will" and awareness.

If you can become meek enough to admit your "lostness," I

guarantee you will be led like a child into the Kingdom of Heaven found in the present moment.

Sir William Osler said, "No man rises higher than he who knows not whither he is going." Let that always be your attitude and you will remain teachable.

#4. Be vigilant for the Kingdom

Of all the obstacles to success on this path, the biggest is the lack of discipline or mental laziness. Being satisfied with the old ways of reacting because they have worked good enough will be your biggest temptation to overcome. Fortunately, one of the fruits of the Holy Spirit that you receive as you knock on the door of Heaven is self-control. The more you surrender, the more tender the mercy of discipline you will receive. It is one of the very real ways you will recognize the supernatural working in your life.

If you find something that is interfering with your vigilance, cut it off, lop it off. Jesus used those hyperboles in the Bible to bring home His point. "Should your right eye offend you, pluck it out, should your right hand offend you, cut it off." In other words, keep your eye on Jesus and do not allow yourself to be distracted from Him. I do not mean the body's eye but what the ancients call the spiritual eye. To see with this new eye requires you to begin to question the accuracy of that sense organ that you have grown so accustomed to delivering to you an accurate picture of the world you are living in. Although its workings are fabulously complex and elegant, it is prone to error just as your other senses may be, especially when the world you are looking at is restricted to your own desires and preferences. This is called observer bias.

You see what you want to see. The magic shows in Las Vegas rely on just that. In medicine, we talk about how your attitude colors your vision. "All looks yellow that the yellow spy, all looks jaundiced to the jaundiced eye." Stinkin' thinkin' results in a stinkin' life experience. Stinking lives come from many days and moments of stinking thinking. You see what you expect to see as you write and rewrite with your own judgment the script of your own little melodrama.

You will develop new vision given as a gift from the Guide and imparted to you simply as a result of a tiny, not yet complete, willingness to see things differently. It will grow to replace the rather restricted worldview delivered to you by your five senses. You will still use your biological mechanisms, but the origin of the stimulus will come from within rather than from without.

Vigilance involves recognizing the early signs of fear. When you feel a pang of discomfort in your chest, unease in your stomach, palpitations in your heart, vow to see this emotional trigger differently. If you persist in asking, I promise you will be answered with a new way of seeing things.

#5. Forgiveness is the tool for all encounters.

Above, I noted the need for vigilance for the Kingdom. Melanie, like many of my other patients as well as myself, at times felt a loss of control over her thoughts. She believed that somebody else was in control of the yes/no part of her brain. In a way she is correct. She was listening to the voice of the little self, or as the psychologists call it, the ego. I like to call it the devil or Satan because those words have a much longer history and connote a much more crafty and powerful opponent. We made this voice up over many years, unwittingly to take the place of God. We started relying on it in early childhood as the source of judgment of the good and bad in our everyday lives, and before long, we forgot our role in its contrived existence so that it appears to take on a life of its own. It is our own little god come to take the place of our real Creator. Thus we come to the insane conclusion that we created ourselves. That idea is so disconcerting, we cannot tolerate it. So we disassociate from it; thus, the "somebody else" that seems to be in control of our thoughts and the yes/no part of our brains. Remember the Great Battle we discussed; you have to admit you are in control of your thinking.

This is not just some isolated mental sleight of hand, but pretty much the case with most everybody walking about Planet Earth today.

That really is why you must make your mantra, "I will forgive because I have been forgiven." This must become your response to every encounter with your fellow travelers. Furthermore, it must become your response especially to those you think have "done you wrong." Not just some of the time, but all of the time. The thought of forgiveness is to be the Holy Grail of your life.

I tell you again, you must include every living thing in your circle of holiness, if you are to experience present-moment living. Otherwise, you are trapping yourself in the past with your brothers. You are guaranteeing that your future and that of your brothers will be just a repeat of what went on before. You will keep on reacting to them just like you did before. You have to see them in a new light if you are to see yourself in a new light. The message of the cross was meant for the entire world, not just you and a few of your select family and friends. Please, no doctrine here. I am speaking to you and what you must do to live in the present moment. Your thinking is ultimately the only thing over which you have control. Not the other guy's.

As I said before, this all-encompassing type of forgiveness for everyone does not come naturally. It must be learned. The best that you can expect of your biology is to "forgive" selectively. The forgiveness I am referring to is the supernatural ability that is your gift from the Holy Spirit. You make room for it as you give up your old ways of looking at things in the context of your own restricted melodrama.

#6. Be a friend of the world

Membership in restrictive groups that are based on exclusionary doctrine carries a hazard to present-moment living. It breeds that "us and them" mentality. Subtly, it lends a "specialness" to your particular viewpoint and can cause you to be quite defensive about your particular position. The thought that you have something to defend leads you to feel unsafe and pushes you to thinking into the future where you believe loss may occur. Although material wealth is the most prominent when considering "fear of loss," other less-obvious but equally peace-disruptive things like social positions, religious doctrines, political philosophies, and materialism pull you inexorably away from the "here and now." Your desire to be right in your judgments compels you to seek out others with similar views. It tends to reinforce itself as you seek safety in numbers.

Melanie had developed fears for the safety of the world and found herself becoming angry at rather abstract groups that she felt threatened her way of life. I do not challenge the fact you <u>can</u> worry about the state of world events. I do challenge you that your worry has any positive benefits in changing them for the better. As long as you persist in having the idea that the world is out to get you or your group, you cannot experience present-moment living. What is important is that you become the world's friend and the only way to do this is to forgive first and then you will understand. Not the other way around. You will be given understanding as you give up your judgment of world events.

In an "us" versus "them" world, your biology will restrict the scope of your forgiveness to your immediate friends and family. That is the size of a clan or about one hundred to a hundred and twenty-five people. Sometimes, with the manipulation of your frontal lobes, you might extend the "us" and "them" to your national borders. Jesus, however, is asking for much more than that. He is asking you to extend it to your enemies. There is no longer any "us" and "them." There is only "us" in the world he invites you to behold. And from personal experience, I can tell you it is a lovely world.

I continue to see a large number of elderly patients in particular who, for a whole host of reasons, are upset about the "sad state" our world is in. You might remember Chad from Chapter 1, who felt that the world was going to hell in a handbasket. Very frequently, this attitude morphs into anger, especially toward other groups of different skin color, political persuasion, ethnicity, or religious beliefs. News media take advantage of the tendency by keeping things stirred up by playing on the fears and manipulating them for better ratings and advertising revenues.

At least for a while, I am asking you to minimize your contact with the more incendiary of these sources until you have gained some real day-to-day experience with the use of forgiveness in your immediate surroundings and social contacts.

When I first began this program in earnest over twenty years ago, I gave up all TV and radio news. I stopped reading the newspapers cover to cover. I vowed I would not read a newspaper unless the headlines of all three of the dailies we received in Nacogdoches were in agreement as to the most important news. Guess what? In a year, not one time did they all carry the same headline. You have enough to focus on with your children, spouses, parents and co-workers. Eventually, as you do the work close to home, you will discover your attitude toward the world becoming a much friendlier one. You will note more people are kinder to you, your way becomes smoother, more people smiling. This is the world you experience through your five senses, not the one delivered by external sources such as television, computers, or even social networking sites such as My Space or Facebook. Your Guide will guide you in your ordinary life to see a new, much friendlier place rising to take the place of the scary world of the past and future you have been limiting yourself to. Eventually, you will be able to resume these sources of "communication", but I promise you they will not stir you up as they did before you received your new sight.

#7. **Do not seek happiness (pleasure)**

Happiness as used in today's world is really pleasure, not the joyful, deep peace that leads to an outward expression of an inward working. Pleasure is dependent upon external circumstances usually related to some temporary stimuli to the pleasure centers of your brain. Money, drugs, eating, shopping, and exercise are just a few of the idols we mentioned before that you might use in your pursuit of "happiness." It usually does not work, at least for long.

There is a great scene in Jerry Bruckheimer's recent film, *The Confessions of a Shopaholic,* when the character Becky says, "Why do I shop? It makes the world look better for a while, then not," she ruefully concludes.

"Seek and do not find" is the mantra of this material world. The pursuit of the idols or forms restricts and constrains your behavior to the biological limits of the body. They all have in common the temporary stimulation of the pleasure center in the limbic part of the brain which has been shown experimentally to always ultimately fail and sooner or later produce real physical pain.

Recall Chapter 4 where we discussed the different "centers" in your brain. Remember that the Grinch will eventually steal the Christmas you are trying to achieve by your stimulation of your pleasure center in your own brain.

The false sensation of "all is great at this moment" will always be followed by the ***down***. This will always occur if you are using external means to try to bring you to the present moment.

For example: We can take the monkey we experimented on

earlier and place an electrode into the pleasure center of the limbic portion of its brain. We can then allow the monkey to press a lever that stimulates this area. The monkey gets really carried away and exhibits some very compulsive lever-pushing activity. He likes it. So compulsive is this behavior, if we now give the monkey a choice of pressing that lever or a separate lever that delivers food, the monkey goes for the feel-good lever. Sometimes, the monkey will continue to do this to the exclusion of eating and drinking, ultimately resulting in death. Not always, but occasionally. In medicine, we see this behavior particularly in the case of some drug addictions, especially amphetamines and cocaine. Methamphetamine addiction is the worst. It gives the illusion of present-moment living when it, in fact, is hastening the death of the body. Addicts pleasure themselves to death.

With your pursuit of some of the more socially acceptable idols, you are still stimulating this same pleasure center. In all cases, you are restricting your worldview to the biology of the brain and its desires.

The gift of joy or true happiness is not dependent upon external stimuli. It comes from within and is one of the gifts of the Holy Spirit. It is a byproduct of living in the present moment. I, quite frankly, do not know if it works through the same center of my brain as the other idols do. I do know that the joy is not followed by the *down* of the false gods.

Joy is the natural consequence of giving up the past and placing the entire future in the hands of the loving Father. It is an outgrowth of the corrected perception of the world offered by your willingness to try forgiveness rather than judgment as your first, second and third reaction to any discomforting want.

Paradoxically, joy comes when you stop pursuing happiness as a goal. It comes by accepting the fact you have everything you need, right in this NOW.

#8. Anger is never justified

This is probably the hardest pill my patients, you and I have to swallow. It is difficult because we have had so much practice over the years, we have trouble giving up our right to be defensive about something. When I say anger is never justified, I am referring to your ultimate place in reality and the sovereignty of the Creator's will.

It has its origins in our disappointment that the happenings of the world are not turning out like we expected.

The visible world is what it is, and your anger, you must remember, is a mask for fear and will not change anything, but will instead only cloud your experience of it.

The saying that you can either fight or flee is not complete. You can also flow. That is the lesson of the ancient Zen masters story told earlier. Otherwise, you will allow your autonomic nervous system to dictate your responses to life's events. Anger and its accompanying physical effects of increased heart rate, elevated blood pressure, and flushing of the skin is generally so uncomfortable that we learn fairly early on in our development to suppress the awareness of the most obvious symptoms. We also become adept at <u>not</u> recognizing the external cues. As a result, most people do not recognize how seething inside they have become. By becoming angry, you, in effect, are saying: "I am unsafe, I feel threatened, I have identified with my body; God is not in control and I have something or believe something that requires my defense." Do you remember those two episodes of rage I described? On reflection, I realized that I was defending something in both cases, my honor. It was my ego I was defending.

All these thoughts are in fact delusional. That is why I would not agree with Kirk, who had a physical fight with his father, that he was justified in his anger.

To those of you who would cite religious indignation as the

exception to the above rule, let me assure you it is not so. You are to be always in the present moment, and righteous indignation only leads you to error someplace else, that is, the past or the fear that the future will look just like the past. Do not confuse zeal with anger. Having strong principles does not require you to be angry if somebody else does not agree with you. This simply puts them as well as you on the defensive.

I have no better thought on how to correct angry thoughts than the timeless advice of Helen Schucman and William Thetford in the book, *A Course in Miracles*, which states: *Nothing real can be threatened, nothing unreal exists.*

Your anger is your attempt, always ultimately unsuccessful, to make your illusions real. Anger and its physical consequences upon the body certainly speed up its dissolution and result in much pain and suffering. Later, we will discuss anger and its effects on your immune system.

Melanie and I discussed her plans to implement these rules for present-moment living in her life. Her very real, not theoretical life.

I am not sure how far Melanie will proceed down the narrow road that leads to life. It is a hard road and Melanie, unfortunately, is like the monkey experiment I noted above. It is quicker and easier to reach for the pill to ease fears temporarily, but I promise you there will always be the *down.*

Short-term, there is a place for the use of tranquilizers. Most commonly, I use them to help somebody who has had the sudden loss of a loved one to help them rest for a few nights.

Chronic use of tranquilizers results in destroyed lives. It trivializes the experience of life and promotes a lie that you are helpless and, what is more, that true help is not available. The problem is in no way confined to non-believers, as Melanie's case so correctly points out. The devil will give you a substitute for real present-moment living and he will play to your weaknesses of laziness and lack of self-control to keep you believing that you cannot see the open door to your jail cell.

In the next chapter, we will discuss how the focus on quantity of calendar years can rob you of a rich and surprising life of the continual present that a forgiving heart can give you. By not holding the past against your brother, you can wake up in a new world every day.

By not focusing on the future years, you will eliminate a whole host of unproductive worries. I know because I spent a huge amount of my time trying to extend my own biological limit of one hundred and twenty years. The joke was on me and those poor souls who came to me for advice on the best plan to get it done.

Chapter 7

So You Want To Be 120

The basis of all health, sinlessness, and immortality is the first fact that God is the only Mind; and this Mind must be not merely believed, but it must be understood.
          Mary Baker Eddy, Founder of Christian Science

All knowledge is infinite in detail; therefore, our understanding of it must always remain superficial.
          La Rochefoucauld, French moralist, philosopher

In the last chapter we focused on the present moment as being the most important time in your daily activities. I believe your awareness of the possibility of eternal life began with Jesus's resurrection two thousand years ago. You and I, if we believe what happened, can throw away our clocks. Now I know that sounds silly and impractical, but that is the implication of His promise.

I have already told you that I think Jesus is and was the smartest man in the world. He knew that his getting up on the third day after he was crucified would stand "science" on its head.

If you remember in Chapter One, I confessed I had worshiped the god of knowledge. This started in late high school, and extended through college and medical school. The facts or "truths" I esteemed had been largely garnered through the "scientific method." I had come to trust those facts almost without question. You will also recall that my clinging to this view or interpretation of events led to my *Rock of Gibraltar* award. It was an extremely important turning point in my life because of the lesson of humility. I did not totally give up my confidence, but I did begin to question how I and my teachers came to believe what we believed. In keeping with our habit of defining our terms, let us make sure we continue to see "eye to eye".

Empiricism: *a disregarding of scientific methods and relying solely on experience.*   Webster's Dictionary

Scientific method: *designating the method of research in which a hypothesis, formulated after systematic, objective collected data, is tested empirically.*   Webster's Dictionary

I have defined these terms for you so that it is very apparent that, ultimately, "scientists" are going to have a problem. The testing of scientific hypotheses or theories is done empirically. This testing will always require an observer and the observer cannot avoid bias. The bias can take many forms to include, but not be limited to, financial, intellectual, gender, educational, religious, emotional, political, national, instrumental, and yes, even genetic issues.

My point is that you and I can only have our opinions. We cannot know scientific facts for sure in the branch of science called medicine. Like it or not, medicine as it is practiced today worldwide is an empirical undertaking. Moreover, because the subjects, you and I, have so many confounding variables, it is extremely difficult to extrapolate from the results they get in the labs and clinical research centers across the world to the individuals who walk into the medical offices of their personal physicians.

Thus, I have found myself gradually becoming more and more empirical in my approach to those seeking my help. If something works, and, in my opinion is not likely to do permanent harm, I will use it. As I have alluded to before, and you will see below, spiritual issues as well as diet and exercise form the basis of most of the opinions I render daily in my medical practice. Certainly, for diet and exercise, science has given its seal of approval. Spiritual issues are another matter where science is concerned, but, it has not always been so.

In Jesus's day, the "scientists" were the learned priestly class, the Pharisees. They were also the "physicians" of their day. If you became ill, you would wash yourself in some pool of water and then would show yourself to the priest, who made a sacrifice of some kind for you, using the rules and regulations found in the Old Testament. This was done for venereal diseases, skin problems like leprosy, and gynecologic problems, as in excessive menstrual bleeding, just to name a few. They were the empirical scientists and physicians of their time. To treat a medical problem, they tried something and waited to see if the patient improved. That is called empiricism by some, quackery by others. The Pharisees certainly thought they had the visible world pretty well figured out. They relied on their outward experience.

Then comes an uneducated Judaean peasant who does some phenomenal things that seemed to speed up the healing process to a degree they had never seen before. It was as if this carpenter had learned some kind of magic to control time. This shook their worldview so much that they correctly saw Him as a real threat to their power structure. So they killed Him.

However, this is not the end of the story. He got up out of the grave, thus totally blowing the concept of linear time out of the water. Not just for the five hundred or so people who saw Him in those first forty days of the new never ending-clock, but for you and me as well.

You and I cannot truly say we believe Jesus is and was who He said He was and still hang onto our old concepts of time. By doing so, we are trying to live in two worlds at the same time and this will always produce unease, fear and a split mind.

C.S. Lewis in his famous book, <u>*Mere Christianity*</u>, has a wonderful chapter on time and beyond time in which he attempts to explain the concept of timelessness. I think he does a nice job with a difficult topic. I agree with him that understanding timelessness is not essential to Christian beliefs; however, I do feel understanding and living as if time no longer mattered will do enormous good if it helps to rid you of the fear of death.

We are going to look at the concept of time and timelessness where your true spirit identity is. We will also look at the physical body, which is not timeless but can be a useful tool. Next, we will review some of the errors the "scientists" of our day are making, just like the Pharisees of old. Even if they have trouble admitting it, they are functionally empiricists, which says they are relying on their personal experiences to define the world as it appears to them. I know because I am and have been one as well. Finally, saving the best for last, I am going to bring to your attention an example of a body existing outside all the laws of "science" that we worship today.

You may ask, what does the desire to live to the ripe old age of 120 have to do with fear and a forgiving heart? It has everything to do with the battle that is going on in each and every one of us as to our true identity. As I told Melanie, her answers to the three questions: Who am I? Why am I here? And What am I supposed to do? will determine whether she will emerge from her prison of fears.

The desire to live a "long life" or win the contest of most years on Planet Earth often carries with it an unstated illusion that you are your body. That is an error that must be corrected if you are to make progress on the path of awakening to the new forgiven world that I want you to see. As long as you identify with your body, you will be afraid, you will be defensive and you will attack. No exceptions.

The Neutral Body

The body is a neutral participant in the war waged within you. In and of itself, it is unimportant. Understanding the neutrality of the body is of prime importance in understanding the origin of many - if not most - physical illnesses. The body ultimately does what it is directed to do by your mind and, shocking as it might appear at first thought, your mind is not confined to your brain. I know this is quite a leap in your awareness, but the brain exists in your mind, not the other way around. You are not your brain. It is a wonderful part of your communication skills, but it is not you.

Although I do not agree with the Frenchman, Rene Descartes, on everything, he certainly saw accurately the neutrality of the body in this observation in 1644: "The principal effect of the passions is that they incite and persuade the mind to will the events for which they prepared the body." *Les Passions de l'ame*

Although most would deny it, we act as if the body were in control of us rather than the other way around. Your thinking can ultimately direct the actions of your body. You have subconscious thinking as well as conscious thinking as we have seen before. When I say your thinking, I am including both types.

If your body is used for communication with your brothers only, it will serve you quite well and requires only a certain amount of maintenance. If, however, you identify with it as being who you are, then you will use it for one or all of the following three things: for show, for pleasure or for attack. In other words, if you choose to identify with the ego or the devil, you will also choose to identify with your body as an ally. You will restrict your experiences to your biological drives, or as Descartes puts it, your passions.

Let me give you an example of this neutral body principle to illustrate the amazing innate self-healing of the neutral body in the medical condition known as "brain death." Many of the body's functions continue without any apparent thinking at all.

Brain Dead Body Experiment

There are strict criteria for defining brain death which are meant to confirm the permanent cessation of the higher cortical centers. The body in this condition is said to be in a vegetative state. If a medical team provides adequate nutrition and fluids, the body can remain in homeostasis for quite some time, months, even years. Here, I am referring to those parts of the body still working.

If you make an incision in this individual to repair or to remove an organ, the wound will heal very nicely. If a bacteria gains access to the bloodstream or urinary tract, for example, the body will mount a vigorous defense response in order to protect the whole body, minus the non-functioning parts of the brain. This is a very intricate and coordinated action and, in most instances, is quite effective in protecting the integrity of the remaining structures. Physiologists would say these coordinated actions of the different parts of the body are designed to protect and maintain homeostasis, each part playing a role in the harmonious working of the whole body.

You can alter this homeostasis by introducing large doses of the hormone cortisol (one of the stress hormones). The body will not heal as well if an incision is made. Why? Because the immune system is involved in healing and has now been compromised with the introduction of steroids interfering with the natural working of this immune system. If you inject epinephrine, the blood vessels will constrict, blood pressure will rise, and the heart will beat stronger and more rapidly because that is what those neutral parts of this neutral body are programmed to do. You do not have to have a brain for these effects to occur. Amazing that absent a good portion of the brain, the body does a pretty impressive job of protecting homeostasis. Now let us add back the rest of the brain, which can be considered a large neuroendocrine organ, and the body truly does an amazing job at maintaining homeostasis. This is what you see in the medically induced coma. In certain traumatic injuries, doctors eliminate the conscious portions of the brain with drugs in order to suppress pain, but the body maintains much of its own functions without the intrusions of thought. It behaves in a neutral manner.

The body will do what the mind directs it to do. Otherwise, it will maintain homeostasis until it receives other orders or signals to do otherwise. Homeostasis is that neutral manner or behavior.

Fear of Death

I admit that I spent the large part of my medical career buying into the idea that quantity of years was a worthy goal. Like most physicians and just like most of you, I had a problem dealing with my own mortality. Occasionally, I would allow the three questions to come to my conscious mind, but most often I would suppress them with my busyness. Like Scarlett O'Hara in *Gone with the Wind* , I would think about those things tomorrow. Until I could answer the questions, Who am I, Why am I here, and What I am supposed to do?, I felt it behooved me to stick around as long as I could. My interest in preventive medicine was as much driven by my own fear of death as trying to get my patients to awaken to their own destructive habits. My focus was on the concepts of eating right, getting enough exercise and what vitamins to take. These I thought were inviolable laws of nature or science, and with enough study, I could come up with a successful program. I thought I could prevent the majority of diseases I was seeing in my practice.

In many ways, the current medical care crisis has its origin in our collective fear of death. As long as we as a nation refuse to recognize how much this drives our individual decisions regarding what we are willing to do to eke out a few more calendar years, I despair of finding a solution that does not include rationing by the authorities in charge of paying for it. It matters not if those authorities are elected or appointed public officials overseeing the public purse or heads of private insurance companies tending the companies' coffers. I once believed we needed a national death policy; I now recognize that was wrong. I now believe each of us should come to grips with death and what that means to each of us personally. A national policy on death is not something to be handed down from above but a decision that comes from below. Each of us can help solve the health care crisis immeasurably by overcoming our own personal fear of the "grand illusion," as Samuel Butler calls it.

Otherwise, the identification with the body along with the fear of death will drive the selfish ego to demand more of whatever is available to prolong its illusory existence, no matter the cost to others. It is just the nature of the beast living an isolated existence confined to it own restricted melodrama.

Time: Are We Satisfied with Too Little?

The title for this chapter was actually the title for a second book

I planned to write. This attempt began after my first book *Ultrafit* was published in 1990. At the time, I was intrigued by the whole concept of time, from which we derive our concepts of aging.

I think one of Einstein's greatest contributions to our practical life was his work, which began as just a thought, on the relative nature of this thing called time. Man-made time, or the idea of time, is a powerful illusion. But do not forget that it is just an illusion.

The ideas of space and time were invented by man to deal with the perceived world. Both ideas come from an attempt to relate objects and motion. The earth's motion relative to the sun defines the year. The earth's rotation on its theoretical vertical axis gives us our day. We, in turn, divide our days into hours, minutes and seconds, etc. We have clocks everywhere to remind us of time. Our legislators reinforce the idea of controlling time by passing laws such as daylight saving time, thus reinforcing the illusion and our identification with it. As a way of trying to become less time-dependent, I stopped wearing a watch in 1990. My wife, who is more than enough time-conscious for both of us, laughs and says the reason I can get by without a watch is that she is always available as my clock.

As Einstein pointed out, time is relative to motion. It is not an absolute. It depends on who is observing, and the speed the observer is traveling through another man-made idea, that is space, stellar space.

Practically, for you and me, time is indeed relative. The length of a year appears to be compressed as one ages. How often have you heard, "The older I get, the faster times seem to occur?" The explanation for this seems to be the number of experiences and memories we are using for comparison. A child of seven lives to be eight and compares the years of experiences to the five or so that he can remember so a year appears relatively long to that child. "Are we there yet?" is just a reflection of his perception of the slowness of time. When we are busy, with lots of experiences, time "seems to fly." When we are focused on something intentionally, in a zone so to speak, time seems to disappear. In retrospect, I think that is what happened to me back in that chemistry class in high school. I bet you have had similar experiences.

Modern technology with its illusions of progress has only reinforced this illusion of time and our seeming dependence on it. The whole idea of improving productivity is based on getting more work done in the same time or the same amount of work done in less time. This is carrying the illusion of time too far. I frequently see people who work on a production line and get high blood pressure trying to keep up.

As a physician, I can tell you that hurry can be a lethal disease to the body itself or at least produce some incapacitating problems.

Usually, the person in a hurry is also quite impatient. The nervous system becomes more irritable. Impatience always carries with it hidden anger which, we have noted before, is just morphed fear. Fear of what? Not getting our own way. Our own will appears out of sync with the ways of the universe. It is a simple case of my melodrama versus the competing melodrama of others. It is the opposite of where you need to be heading. Remember the elevated cholesterol in the accountants on or around April 15th of each year? Their sense of hurry was a big part of the cause of their high cholesterol number.

We have already talked about fear's effects on the blood pressure and stress hormones. It is not a big jump in reasoning to see what the illusion of time can do to the body's efforts at homeostasis. When you have the sense of hurry, which will frequently reveal itself as a sensation of flushing,(particularly the ears), palpitation or irregular heart beat or muscle tension across the upper back or shoulders, you can know that you have indeed been caught up in the world's melodrama. You have identified with its offerings as you frantically seek satisfaction where it cannot be found. Remember, in the previous chapter, these are your cues that you are not being vigilant for the present moment.

Over the years, I have noticed that each of us has our own peculiar signals to warn us we are trying to get too much done at once. The Guide will use your signals to help lead you back to the present moment. Some of my patients get twitching of their eyelids. Others have different little tics. You should become familiar with yours and use it as a sign to slow down.

It's Not Rocket Science, Bob!

For a number of years, my wife and I subscribed to several health newsletters. My patients also brought me theirs. The deeper I looked, the less simple and more confused I became. If you did this, what would it do to that? And so on and so on.

I was beginning to understand firsthand what the French philosopher La Rochefoucauld meant when he said, "All knowledge is infinite in detail." The further I pursued the matter, the less I was sure. I began to realize that the "natural health" proponents were just as guilty as the medical profession of building up an artificial body of knowledge that was losing sight of the whole.

I finally had to declare a truce with a friend of mine in the health food business. I told her I would not try to convince her of my "story" if she would not try to convince me of hers.

Let me share a case with you to show you how far this sort of "greediness" for this life can go.

Due to my long interest in preventive medicine, I probably have attracted a disproportionate number of people focused on the quantity side of the aging experience. Most of the time, they leave my office slightly, if not wholly, disappointed, and at times downright upset when I refuse to buy in to their fears of death evidenced by their increasingly complicated approaches to the maintenance of the neutral body's function.

Bob came to see me not long ago. He was a 55-year-old successful attorney, who admitted in our initial interview he had no physical complaints but sought my help with a different problem. He was interested in living a long time, perhaps indeed to 120. It was immediately clear he was well-read, perhaps too well-read, on the issue of "life extension." He subscribed to a number of current newsletters published by, in many cases, our most famous medical teaching institutions. He normally had an executive physical each year costing him a few thousand dollars, but since the typed report he received each of the last four years looked very computer-generated and suspiciously "boilerplate," to use his term, he thought he would seek my advice. Cost was no object as he invited me to draw whatever tests I needed to help guide him on his quest.

"Of course you will check my homocystine, DHEA and highly sensitive C-Reactive protein levels, won't you?," he counseled as well as asked. "How valuable do you think growth hormone, insulin-related growth factor (IGF) and free testosterone levels would be for me?" he added without missing a beat. "If there are any vitamin levels you think would help me, let's get them while I am here; I came fasting just so we could get this done in a timely fashion," he almost comically ended his suggestions of how I might be of help.

After showing me a list as well as the actual sack of the vitamins and nutritional supplements he was currently taking, he gave me a chance to respond.

"Bob, you told me earlier you were a believer, didn't you?" I started my game of stealthily stalking my unsuspecting quarry. "You bet. My wife and I belong to the Baptist church here in town. I rarely miss. By the way, did you know attending church regularly may help you to live longer?" he added without a hint of irony in his voice as he added the last observation.

"Are you any good at math?" I coaxed him a little further down the primrose path I was headed.

"It wasn't my favorite subject, but it didn't keep me out of law school," he replied.

"Then before we go any further with testing and exams, solve this equation for me," I said as I pushed a piece of paper in front of him.

He looked at me quizzically as he pondered the following:

$$\frac{120}{\text{Eternity}}$$

"How big is the numerator Bob?" I asked, after allowing him a few moments to think.

"A very small number," he replied.

"How small?" I pushed on.

"Very, very small," he now came back with an actual quieting of his voice as the truth dawned on him.

"How big is the top number, Bob? That's how long you want to live."

"It doesn't exist!" he almost shouted, as disappointment quickly followed by relief washed across his face. His eyes lit up as our common guide now entered the discussion, confirming His presence in me by a pleasant tingling of the skin of my legs and arms.

I told Bob, and I tell you, the equation is just a symbol of the battle I noted in Chapter Two. The finite cannot be divided by the infinite. Our minds have trouble holding two contradictory thoughts at the same instant. You have to make a choice between which is real and true or what is an illusion and untrue. As a sentient being, you are choosing every instant which of these two choices is true for you.

An interesting phenomenon reveals itself when I query the players in this mind game as to which of the two symbols they believe is real. Almost invariably, the answer is eternity. This is true even with professing atheists. Sometimes the latter get a little angry at my attempt at humor, but, like it or not, they usually concede that eternity, or the infinite, is more pleasing to the mind when they consider it. It just seems to resonate somewhere, somehow deep within.

It is my opinion it resonates precisely because the Creator has placed eternity in our hearts from the beginning, safe and unchanging. He placed the knowledge of Him; He gave us the gift of knowing Him when we mentally separated ourselves from Him in the garden. His Sovereign Will is that we know Him even though we have mentally fooled ourselves into believing we are apart from Him.

I have told you the story of Bob to illustrate an extreme example of the identification with the body and the real hubris that is involved in going down this slippery slope. The belief that you can manipulate one or a few of the observable or measurable numbers that describe the body supports a huge part of the medical and health food industries. The law of unintended consequences also proves it is quite naive.

Bob's case is also an excellent lesson for professing Christians who commonly avow, "Doc, sure I want to go to heaven, just not right now." By their own admission, they are saying that the battle is not really resolved and they are prepared to "live" in the material world while still dreaming of Heaven to come, awaiting death as if it answers something. It answers nothing.

Before I tell you what I advised Bob to do, let me give you some examples of the fallacy of using the so-called scientific method to extrapolate from the particular to the general. It seems we still have "Pharisaic scientists" in the medical profession today.

The Lesson of Cholesterol

The number-one reason for the body to cease to be of use as an instrument is heart disease, particularly coronary heart disease. The latter is frequently, but not always, the result of the gradual buildup of fatty deposits in the lining of the heart's own primary blood supply. When the fatty plaque is chemically analyzed, cholesterol along with a lot of other things, including white blood cells, were found in high concentration. So scientists postulated a theory that cholesterol must have something to do with the blocked arteries. So far, so good.

Concurrently with these biochemical observations, epidemiologic studies originating in Framingham, Massachusetts, found that people who had heart attacks were most commonly linked by the observable behavior of smoking and the measurable presence of an elevated cholesterol and high blood pressure when compared to those who had not suffered a heart attack.

Fresh out of medical school, confronted with chronic diseases, I honed in on these factors, driven as much by my own limitations in understanding the pathophysiology of this particular disease as much as anything else. It was and is a simplistic approach and it is also quite wrong. It is wrong because it is too simple an answer for a multi-factorial problem where we can only assess risk not certainty. Remember, I told you about 10 percent of people who die of a classical myocardial infarction have no chronic cholesterol-type blockage. Something else is going on in at least some of these patients.

There are certain genetic abnormalities characterized by extremely high levels of cholesterol which, if untreated, lead to death at an early age from blockage of these arteries. Treatment of these rare problems became much easier with the basic science work of Nobel Prize-winning Joe Goldstein and Michael Brown and the subsequent development of the statin drugs. In high doses, the statins effectively block the liver's manufacturing of cholesterol at a very early step in its formation. The arrogant intellectual extrapolation from treating these rare individuals to treating the general populace was something I was guilty of and now repent.

If you have high cholesterol, there is a very good chance somebody has tried to put you on these drugs, regardless of whether or not you have had a heart attack.

We are now aware that coronary disease is not a single entity but a complex, often inflammatory process. It is much more complicated than we initially thought. Remember Nickie? I told her that cholesterol can be a marker for stress as well as "poor genes."

My idea of preventive medicine was to push diet, exercise and stress management. When that was ineffective, I, like so many of my colleagues, reached for the prescription pad and began writing prescriptions for those statin drugs, applying them to shakier and shakier clinical encounters that were quite distant from the rare genetic defect Dr. Goldstein described in his initial studies.

A wake-up call occurred one morning a few years ago as I was making hospital rounds. I was in the room of one of my patients and noticed he was watching a news show on which a prominent cardiologist was being interviewed. It was concerning the benefits of statin drugs in lowering cholesterol. The physician's remark both startled me and sickened me. "Statin drugs are so helpful we should put them in the general public's water supply," he said. It took that patently absurd statement to awaken me from my self-induced mental coma and recommit my clinical practice to that age-old adage (I am talking Greek B.C. Hippocrates time): *Primum non nocere* (First, do no harm!).

I am using cholesterol here as an example of a much more important principle. The really good scientists know this to be true. Their voice wisely counseling to beware of extrapolating isolated data to the general population is drowned out by the rush to do something. The fear that there is something wrong drives the demand by people and the drug companies are only too happy to oblige. Medicine is rife with examples of simplistic thinking and, cumulatively, it is breaking the nation's banks, our banks. We are borrowing from ourselves and our children to pay for these errors in our thinking.

The more treacherous fact is this: In our striving to make the body last longer, to eradicate those very same chronic illnesses that cause so much pain and suffering, we may, in fact, play into the devil's hands. The seeking after good health can become an idol. Selfishness is the father of all sin, which I define as separation from God. Our very greed to have more of whatever it is, including more years for our neutral body, is leading us into a moral dilemma for which there is no secular answer. With its innocent face of treating illnesses with increasingly complex technology provided by the use of the "scientific method," medicine is subtly drawing us deeper into a reliance on it for answers rather than our Guide. More and more, we are relying on the five senses to paint our picture of the real world.

Let me stop here for a moment and give you two more examples of rushing to extrapolate from isolated observations to the general population - you and I and our friends.

Beta-carotene, a carotenoid found in high concentrations in

human tissues, has been thought to be an antioxidant. In lay terms, it was thought to keep you and me from rusting out too quickly. That is what antioxidants do.

Carotenoids are plant pigments that protect plant cells from damage. They are the chemicals that make pumpkins and carrots orange and squash yellow.

A large study involving 18,000 people, was conceived to test the effects of beta-carotene and vitamin A in smokers or people who had been exposed to asbestos. The thinking was that by taking an isolated chemical, beta-carotene, and using it in pill form, you could expect a decrease in lung cancer.

You can probably guess what happened. After four years of treatment, the treatment group had a 28% <u>higher</u> incidence of lung cancer than the non-treatment group. The death rate from cardiovascular disease was 26% higher in the treatment group. They stopped the study early.

I am using this example to drive home the point that the neutral body's natural state is homeostasis. With extremely complex biological systems, like the neutral body, "science" has to be very careful about drawing conclusions regarding the efficacy of a proposed, seemingly innocuous thing, like taking a vitamin pill. It is the law of unintended consequences writ large.

As I stated earlier, I once was very sure of myself, particularly in recommending various vitamin combinations to prolong the workings of the neutral body. This is not to say that there is no place for vitamin or nutritional supplements. It is simply a cautionary note for you and me trying to solve our problems with a quickfix instead of working on our own errors in thinking.

A second example of "science" not following the dictum, *primum non nocere,* is to be found in the use of female hormones, especially estrogen replacement therapy.

It is a well-known fact that women have less cardiovascular

disease than men prior to menopause. They are less likely to have strokes or heart attacks than their male counterparts. By age 65, the incidence in both sexes has pretty well evened out.

The Women's Health Initiative was a huge N.I.H. (National Institute of Health) supported study involving billions of dollars. It was thought that the hormone estrogen was responsible, by itself, for the difference in the incidence of cardiovascular disease between the two sexes. Women were started on the hormone replacement therapy at or near their natural menopause. As most of you have seen in the media, the study had to be stopped early due to unexpected high numbers of strokes and heart attacks in the women in the treatment group. At that particular point in their lives, it appears that the ancient wisdom of the neutral body is saying enough is enough. It does not need the extra female hormone that scientific research had thought was the missing link in the puzzle of different gender rates of heart attacks and strokes.

I am using these two examples to reinforce what La Rochefoucauld said concerning all knowledge being infinite in detail and your understanding must always be superficial. The deeper you look, the more mysterious it becomes.

I am pointing out these things to help you in your efforts at present-moment living we discussed in Chapter Six.

I believe you and I will be happiest when we maintain an attitude of reverential awe as we jointly experience this thing we call life. I truly believe that was our state of being in the garden before we bit the apple. In Chapter Two, I referred to one of the symbols of the battle going on in each of our minds in choosing to have, or choosing to be. Most of you may have thought I was referring to material possessions when I said "having." It certainly is true that cars, houses, money, jewelry and so on can be possessed, but so can knowledge. That is to say, we can treat knowledge as a possession. I have had to guard against this idol for much of my life, and I can assure you, and my wife would confirm, I have not always been successful.

If you approach your life moment-by-moment, you will remain teachable, as I pointed out in the last chapter. You will also be less likely to be drawn into future speculation about the continued well-being of the neutral body. You will not be as apt to think that a medicine, or a supplement, or a hormone, or anything outside your own thinking is going to fix you. I have said repeatedly, science can treat your symptoms, but it cannot fix your problems or win the battle of your identity. That has already been done.

How Much Care Is Enough?

Your body, viewed as an instrument of communication, requires very little care - a lot less care than I promoted for most of my medical career, as it turns out. If it is used for show, pleasure or attack in the service of the little self, then its destruction will be hastened. Sow to the flesh, reap to the flesh.

In thirty-seven years of practice, I still believe if you eat right, exercise and learn to handle stress in a constructive manner, the body will not get sick very often. For years, I listed stress management last in order of importance in my talks with groups or individual patients. As you might guess, having read this far, I no longer hold to this priority list. In fact, without addressing the last, stress management, in a most profound way, I am using the first two, diet and exercise, as a way to prevent or delay asking you the most pressing question: Why are you afraid?

How far did I take my idea of preventive medicine? Notice, I said I. My own ego was so wrapped up in how I could fix "medicine" that after eleven years in our small town, I set out to try to do just that. I now recognize that was a symptom of grandiosity, as the devil whispered in my ear: "Sure you can."

I told myself that if I could just get people to focus on the positive things that contribute to the blessing of "good health," then they would not get sick as often. After eleven years, I was tired of dealing with sickness.

Over the next several years, my associates and I built several preventive medicine centers. The central focus was attention to exercise and diet. When it came to stress management, our clients were largely left to their own devices. My usual recommendations on dealing with stress were music, hobbies, exercise, and, almost under my breath, prayer. In order not to offend the perceived sensibilities of our paying customers, I left the selling of God to the church, where I thought it more properly belonged. I did have the insight to remind our staff that, even though what we were selling was an approximation of the truth, it was not the truth itself. It was not the truth about illness and its prevention. It was just better than the traditional "sick care" approach I had been hawking my first eleven years of clinical practice. I conceded then as I concede now that the more you are identified with your neutral body and this world, then the closer you will have to adhere to the first two of the three pillars of preventive medicine.

For example, if you are angry, fearful, hate your job and co-workers, and think this world is out to get you, like Chad, then you darn sure better pay close attention to what you eat and how much exercise you get.

Likewise, if you have the most cherished of all gifts, having found God, have the power of the Holy Spirit and are serving Him, then I do not have to tell you not to worry about what you eat or how much exercise you get. You already know it. And, if you are happy in your external circumstances, if you love your spouse unconditionally, have children who are Rhodes Scholars, and you see the face of God in all you do, odds are that the medical system will go broke waiting on you to partake of its offerings.

The Curious Case of Therese Neuman

I have included the following case to point out the possibility that there may be examples on this planet today that would cause us to throw out all our nice little theories and laws of nutrition and physiology. This medical case occurred during my lifetime, but I did not personally have Miss Neuman as a patient. However, I think her life history represents an example for us. It should serve as a reminder that man truly does not live by bread alone.

How little does the neutral body require? Very, very little, it seems to those who take their cues from the unseen real world of the Spirit.

Therese Neuman was a German peasant lady born in Konnersreuth, Bavaria, Germany. She lived a full and quite active life. To say she was a devout follower of Christ is a gross understatement. During her adult life, her neutral body was subjected to a number of stigmata associated with the crucifixion of Christ, including spontaneous wounds of her hands and side. Much has been written of her, but for our purposes, I want to point out the fact that for thirty-five years she lived a devoted life without ingesting any liquid or food other than the Eucharist offered in daily Mass. Her life spanned sixty-four years and was subjected to rigorous observations. Germany was among the world's preeminent scientific countries at that time and she was investigated by some of its most respected physicians. Their conclusion was that she drew her very life from some other source. She claimed that source was Jesus Christ. Other than what she ate and drank in the Mass, she ate or drank nothing.

I believe God gives every generation tender mercies that shatter our unsatisfactory intellectual constructs, such as the laws of thermodynamics, which this peasant woman's life leaves in tatters, humbling those of us still capable of humility.

Every time I am tempted to believe I know anything, I think of this sweet peasant German lady. I hope you will too.

Advice To All the Bobs Out There

"Bob, let me be truthful. Over the years, I have become less and less sure of myself when giving Dr. Joe's opinion on the best preventive medicine plan. If your spiritual life is really in order, I am not sure I have anything important to add to the equation. If your spiritual life is ***not*** in order, I am not sure what I have to say really matters.

"Bob, my advice to you is not rocket science. Good health is really a blessing or a gift bestowed on those who realize where all of life comes from and that they are part of the whole."

Here are my recommendations:

1. Instead of checking your cholesterol again, check your kindness to all your brothers. How forgiving is your heart?

2. Instead of checking your blood pressure, ask yourself: Why as a Christian am I afraid of death?

3. Instead of worrying about what you eat, ask: Whom have I fed?

4. Instead of measuring your testosterone level, ask: How tender am I to my wife?

5. Instead of adding to your pile of supplements, ask: From

whence does my power come?

Bob, the best advice I have for old age is: Honor your father and mother so that your days may be long. Moreover, you cannot afford the luxury of being angry at anybody.

Having a **forgiving heart** is the best way to have a **healthy heart**. It is more important than any prescription drug or supplements you might find.

We have seen how the sin of greed can play itself out in the seemingly innocent pursuit of good health. Let's you and I turn to see how the sin of wrath can destroy the body in ways you may not be aware of.

Chapter 8
Anger and Autoimmune Diseases

I was angry with my friend;
I told my wrath, my wrath did end.
I was angry with my foe;
I told it not, my wrath did grow.

"A Poison Tree" by William Blake

Men must choose to be governed by God or they condemn
themselves to be ruled by tyrants .

-William Penn

Hesitation is the best cure for anger.

Lucas Seneca, Roman statesman and philosopher

If therefore you are presenting your offering at the altar, and there
remember that your brother has something against you, leave your
offering there before the altar, and go your way; first be reconciled
to your brother, and then come and present your offering.

Jesus Matthew 5:23-24

Envy, mockery, contempt, anger, revenge and the other affects
which are related to hatred or arise from it are evil.

Baruch Spinoza

In Chapter Four, we discussed the effects of fear on the immune

115

system of your body. The emotion fear is accompanied by activation of your white cells. Those white cells are built to attack and repair. Remember, I said the neutral body is going to maintain homeostasis as it is programmed to do so. If your body encounters a foreign invader, a nasty staph bug, for example, your white blood cells are going to attack and get rid of it. This process occurs many, many times every day without your thinking or worrying about it at all.

The same thing happens when one of your body's cells escapes its personal growth regulators and potentially becomes a cancerous cell. Your vigilant immune system takes care of this abnormal cell as though it were a foreign invader and stops it in its tracks. Again, this does not require your mental direction. The body is just programmed that way. I think most oncologists would agree that over a person's lifetime his or her immune system gets rid of cancer cells like a good maid cleans house. She does not have to be directed; she just gets the job done.

Now we are going to discuss a group of diseases that arise when that faithful immune system is put on high alert by the patient's incorrect thinking. The incorrect thought is: *I can attack somebody else and not attack myself.*

I am not telling you that every single case of an autoimmune disease has anger or its predecessor, fear, as its origin. I have learned to be skeptical when it comes to the ultimate cause of any disease. I am saying that in my own experience, unresolved anger and grievances are the origin of the majority of the autoimmune diseases that I have treated. Scientists call this observer bias: You see what you are looking for.

I confess I am guilty of this observer bias. As in the last chapter, I admit again to being an empiricist, not totally, but certainly in my medical practice. I mean I am interested, and always have been, in what works to get people "better." I, too, worshiped the "scientific method," particularly when I was studying organic chemistry.

Unfortunately, or fortunately, depending upon your perspective, biological systems, particularly one so elegant as man, have too many variables to be truthfully subjected to the so-called rigors of the "scientific method." They are not as simple as test tube experiments. Remember the unexpected results of hormone replacement and beta-carotene trials we discussed in the last chapter.

As David said in Psalms, "You are fearfully and wonderfully made." He was talking about you and me. He might just as well have said: "You are fabulously complex."

I must also truthfully admit I have never been totally satisfied with the models of the pathophysiology of many diseases. Not the ones I learned in medical school or the ones currently touted by the molecular biologists.

I also want to confess that I believe that genomic medicine is a joke if it is taken to its logical conclusion. The mystery of man will never be totally unmasked by the study of his DNA, and his suffering will never be defined by the abnormalities of his genetic code.

I believe every man is his own laboratory, and by and large, at least as thinking adults, we are responsible for what goes on in that laboratory ourselves.

This chapter is primarily about autoimmune diseases as I single them out to point out another truism. We literally can become our own worst enemies and we can use our own bodies to prove it if we so choose.

Anger: Wrath implies deep indignation expressing itself in desire to punish or get revenge.

Webster's Dictionary

Autoimmune diseases represent a large proportion of the illnesses that a general internal medicine physician sees. This was

117

especially true before the age of specialization resulted in an increased number of rheumatologists. When I opened my practice in 1978 here in East Texas, it wasn't long before I was seeing a large number of these patients being referred to me by the local family practitioners. Included were many cases of rheumatoid arthritis, systemic lupus erythematosus, scleroderma, psoriasis, Sjogren's syndrome, Graves' disease and Hashimoto thyroiditis. All these diseases have the common theme of the body attacking itself. Sometimes the attack appears to be confined to a single organ, such as the joints in rheumatoid arthritis, but quite often involving multiple organs such as lupus. In all these diseases, if you look hard enough, you will find evidence of widespread inflammation.

Common to all these diseases is the feature of self-attack. That is, the neutral body's defense system has gone on the march against its own tissues, including the brain, heart, lungs, skin, joints, liver, kidneys, red blood cells, muscle tissue, pancreas, thyroid gland, adrenal glands and blood vessels. It is as if the cells involved do not recognize their brothers and sisters and are raising holy sand against them, disturbing the homeostasis of the neutral body.

Some of these diseases share enough common features that medical science lumps them into groups and gives them a name. As with coronary heart disease, most of these disease entities are not single, circumscribed problems, but instead are very complex issues with much overlap seen clinically. Naming them frequently requires very expensive exams involving blood work, X-rays and sometimes tissue biopsies.

It would be laughable were it not so expensive to see the battery of blood tests that are ordered in order to pin down a "diagnosis." Early in my career, I remember feeling a sense of self-satisfaction when in seeing a patient in consultation that I was indeed able to label the problem. As noted before, this reinforced my illusion of orderliness in the whole process, the problem fitting neatly into my pre-packaged disease categories.

There are several interesting features of these diseases. First, women suffer from them much more commonly than men (about a ten-to-one ratio). They occur twice as frequently in blacks as compared to whites. They occur more commonly in certain families. If your mother or twin sibling has a problem, you are more likely to develop one, although not the same one, and there appears, as with all illness, a genetic component.

As I have noted earlier, I think your genetic code contributes to how fear and anger make their appearance known to you. Except in rare isolated cases, genes are not the determinant feature, but instead just part of the canvas.

Despite spending huge amounts of research dollars on the effort, science is at a loss to explain the cause or trigger of this auto-attacking phenomena. For over sixty years, they have diligently looked and the cause or trigger is still unknown. I would like to suggest the trigger for these illnesses is frequently anger or fear.

Since the cause remains unknown, the treatment is empirical. There is that word again. The treatment is largely a hit-and-miss proposition. The immune system is too revved up, so we try to tone it down. One of the drugs used is prednisone, a common steroid. It works by interfering with the immune system's function. Drugs that stop immune cells from proliferating also help, particularly those that allow us to use lower doses of prednisone. We have become quite skilled at manipulating different steps in the immune system function. Science and the drug companies have come up with some elegant (from a biochemical standpoint) compounds that block the effects of some of the products produced by the white blood cells. Unfortunately, like the statin drugs, estrogen hormone replacement therapy and beta-carotene, this has been accompanied by the law of unintended consequences. These same immune-modifying drugs interfere with the everyday defense and healing process that your neutral body depends upon for its proper functioning. They are also terribly expensive for the uninsured, and thus help dig us collectively into a deeper and deeper ethical hole. Technology has outstripped our ability as a nation to pay for it, and class warfare is raising its ugly head as we fight to see who gets what and debate who shall pay for it. I am writing this book to help you realize these autoimmune diseases are largely preventable. I think that is very good news. Also, if you suffer from one of these illnesses, you have a much larger role in healing yourself than you might imagine.

A Gradual Awakening

As I mentioned in the last chapter, in 1990 I set out on an ego-driven vision quest to prevent disease and, with a great deal of help, we developed several preventive medicine centers here in the state of Texas. We took all comers. If you were not wheelchair-bound, we had a program for you. We even offered our clients a "Body Warranty" which stated that if you came to our facility and worked out an average of 8 times per month, then your outpatient medical care was free in regard to the physician's time. After eleven years of the traditional approach to sick care, I wanted to see how the system would work with reverse incentives for both the patient and the physician. Over those eleven years, I learned a number of humbling things about the different problems I had been so quick to label during my first years of practice.

Mixed in with this all-comers population were several patients with autoimmune diseases, particularly early rheumatoid disease and lupus. I developed a new attitude. I was not interested in labeling their problem. I was interested in how functional I could help them to be in their lives and how many medications I could get them to eliminate. I decided to really try the empirical method first-hand.

What I discovered was that somehow the act of doing some exercise in some way made them better. It seemed that the changing of the mind of the patient to resolve to get better had gradually allowed the neutral body to do just that. It was as if you were pointing people, not patients, in a new direction, the direction of self-healing. The intent to get well got them well. I stopped treating the sick different from the "well."

As I related earlier, stress management, the most important of my three-prong plan, was not seriously addressed, both due to limitation of resources and my ignorance of its importance in the scheme of things. But many of the patients did get better and rarely did I have to make good on the "Body Warranty". This awakening process was not a sudden epiphany like I referred to earlier; it was more of a gradual dawning. Time after time, the patient was able to give up the idea of victimhood as she took more and more responsibility for the health of her body, not relying on doctors to "fix" her.

Anger and Attack

In earlier chapters, I have made it clear that the best way to view the bodies we seem to inhabit is as neutral bystanders in the war that goes on in our minds.

If you have found God and put the neutral body at the service of the Spirit, then you can expect it to work quite harmoniously. It is programmed to do so without your thinking much about it. One way to look at it is that it is a convenient way to communicate with others. If it is used solely for communication by the Spirit, then your body will communicate only love, for that is what the Spirit is.

If, however, you choose to use the body in the service of your ego or the devil, you will use it for one of three things: attack, show or pleasure. Show means vanity in all its forms. Basically, you are restricting its use to the biological drives. Your body is still neutral; it will do what it is told to do. The telling is most often below your conscious awareness and the body responds very rapidly to these directions. Largely, the directions will flow from your limbic system or the more primitive parts of your brain. Remember, in this perceptual world, you are either *dinner or diner*. As I have discussed earlier, this defense mechanism is very primitive and extremely hard-wired and almost, but not entirely, subconscious. You can learn to recognize your attack thoughts. It is almost as if things were so dangerous in the body's distant past, that to think was to lose valuable time.

Remember Dr. Libet's experiment? You set in motion behaviors before you become aware of it. Remember that 0.3-second delay. You set in motion even volitional acts before you are conscious of having set them in motion. All of the men and women I have interviewed can recall an incident where, to use their own words, before they knew what they were doing, they had physically or at least verbally attacked someone. I certainly know I have; how about you?

As an experiment, I now ask a new patient with any chronic rheumatologic problems to recall how often in any given day they become aware of attack thoughts. It is usually quite an eye-opener for all of us as we realize the frequency. It is usually related to some physical characteristic of the one attacked. She's fat, she's too skinny, he's ugly, he looks mean. She's tall, short. The list goes on but usually does not stop there. It progresses to assigning other negative feelings about those characteristics. You get the picture.

Try it. You are much more likely to do it with strangers; that is just your ancient defensive biology at work. That is the us- against-them phenomenon. That is your judgmental attitude at its worst. This is were xenophobia has its origin.

Now we have looked at both ends of the spectrum: the rare rage or physical or verbal attack and the much more common, seemingly confined to the brain, attack thoughts. However, both of these have physiologic consequences. They both have effects on your immune system as well as the cardiovascular system. This is just a further extension of the idea that your neutral body is going to do what your brain tells it to do.

As we discussed earlier, your neutral body has a very potent and capable immune system which not only wards off offensive single-cell organism invaders but is the key player in healing cuts, scrapes and other traumas. Many of the cues that trigger this anger response vary from person to person and can be manipulated by others tampering with your frontal lobes. The different ways you feel threatened, your cues, depend to a large degree on whether you are male or female. Gender is also responsible for much of the way we express our anger. This is where it gets even more intriguing.

Dealing with Anger - Male vs. Female

Anger, as I noted in Chapter 6, is never justified. It is always due to a fear of loss of something or an incorrect belief in who you are. If you identify yourself as body and not Spirit, then you are much more apt to become angry.

The rage response is much more common in men than women. This is evident in the fact that the majority of violent crimes are perpetrated by men. It does not mean women do not commit violent acts; it is just more common in men. Research suggests that testosterone is a major player in facilitating the brain's response and has large effects on the limbic portion of the brain. Violent acts are more common during the peak testosterone-producing years of sixteen to thirty. Testosterone levels peak at about age thirty-five, remain relatively stable, and then begin to decline around age fifty.

The phenomenon of steroid rage is just an exaggerated effect of normal biology. You see this primarily in males who supplement with the superphysiologic amounts of "knock-off" testosterone. Aggressive behavior can vary from increased sexual activity to increased nervous system instability, including psychosis and rage. These behavioral changes operate through the limbic system of the brain, below conscious awareness. Rage involves so much output of stress hormones that the individual will not be able to tolerate it for long. I remember how lethal the rage response felt when I experienced it. It was not pleasant at all. Remember Kirk, who had the fight with his father. So much release of the stress hormone norepinephrine caused Kirk to become ill, literally wasting away as he lost thirty-five pounds over a very short period of time. This kind of anger decreases the appetite. Have you ever been so mad that it made you sick? That is what is happening here. You can fight or flee, but you do not have time to eat.

Have you ever heard of a person getting so angry they had a heart attack? Hemodynamic effects on the blood supply are probably at work here. Rage increases the stress hormones epinephrine and norepinephrine, increasing oxygen needs of the heart by increasing the strength of the contraction of the heart muscle as well as increasing the heart rate. At the same time, the blood vessels throughout the body constrict, including those arteries supplying blood to the heart muscle itself, cutting off vital blood flow just when it is needed most. Remember the ten percent of people who have heart attacks and normal arteries? Some of these are due to anger. The anger caused the release of norepinephrine, which in turn caused the spasm of the blood vessels supplying the heart. This is not a new observation. John Hunter, a famous English cardiologist, had this to say about angina pectoris (more commonly referred to as chest pain). "Damn this angina pectoris, it puts my life at the mercy of any rogue who would provoke me." That was written in the 1700s. This was pretty insightful back then and still is today.

How many times do you think the topic of anger is raised in the cardiologist's office today when discussing preventive strategies with the patient? Doctors are far more likely to focus on statin drug therapy and beta blockers. Cholesterol levels and blood pressures are easier to measure and deal with than the emotion anger.

Autopsy studies have shown no build-up of fatty material in the lining of the blood vessels of some of these individuals who die suddenly in a fit of rage. Cause of death? It was not heart disease that killed them. It was anger. The neutral body was simply doing what it was programmed to do. Again as reported above, this situation occurs more frequently in males. When the statistics are totaled at the end of the year, this death will be lost among all the rest. This is one extreme example of the heart, as an organ, being blamed for doing what it was told to do by the brain.

What happens if you have rage and the body does not quit working as in our friend whose heart could not handle the anger? What if you just hold on to the anger, the conflict, the grievance, your honor, your "rights," your image of yourself, your social position, etc., whatever has offended you or threatened you and made you feel unsafe? This is a simmering type of anger or, as Dr. Friedman called it, "free floating hostility." In this case, the immune system attacks the lining of the vessels, and in the setting of increased cholesterol, fatty material builds up in the arteries, and you find the classic fatty plaque of chronic coronary heart disease.

This is a simplification, but I believe it explains a large part of the number-one killer of Americans today, heart disease. Although coronary heart disease is not considered a classic autoimmune disease, I believe that autoimmunity plays a key role in initiating and maintaining this "chronic" condition. I tell my heart patients that they cannot afford the luxury of anger. They are paying for this cardinal sin with the destruction of the lining of their blood vessels.

Women Really Are Different

Fear and anger produce uncomfortable physical states when you allow them to rise to your conscious brain. As you suppress the grievance and hold on to the grudge, your body cannot stop the biological effects of this signal to your neutral body. You will activate your immune system, putting it on high alert and taking it away from its normal function of repair and maintenance of homeostasis. Depending on your genetic background, this immune system on high alert can make an "error." It will attack its own tissues and the body begins to slowly eat itself up. This is exactly what happens in autoimmune diseases.

The term "hot-headed" referring to angry thoughts can be translated to a "hot body" or literally, an inflamed body.

It is the socio-biological nature of women to suppress their anger and, as a result, they are much more prone to these autoimmune diseases. This is not a sexist statement, but a fact as well as an observation from my thirty-plus years of practice. Women are simply more likely to hold grudges than their male counterparts, and suppressed anger consumes more mental energy. It is also the reason women suffer from the diagnosis of depression much more frequently than men. We will discuss this in more detail in Chapter 10.

Now let us look at three individuals and how each one reacted to their own anger, resentment and/or grievance. I want to show you the perils of looking to "science" to fix your problem rather than examining your own unforgiving heart.

Maria and the Ungrateful House Guests and Unthoughtful Husband

Maria came to see me to have her blood drawn. About two and a half months before our encounter, she had developed the onset of severe muscle and joint pain. It had started in her hands and spread to her knees and feet. After a few weeks of discomfort, she sought the counsel of her primary care physician. When an initial exam was unrevealing at his office, a referral was made to a neurologist. Likewise, he was unable to find any gross objective findings and ordered a battery of tests, including tests for Lyme disease, lupus, and rheumatoid arthritis, which prompted her to see me.

As I was drawing her blood, unable to resist the temptation to satisfy my curiosity, I inquired, "Maria, when did your symptoms begin?"

Looking a little puzzled, she replied, " Just after Christmas. Three or four days after Christmas. I remember quite well since my birthday is December 24th and it began a few days after that."

Boldly, since I had no prior contact with her, I asked if she minded if I asked a personal question. With her consent affirmed by the nodding of her head, I proceeded.

"Maria, is there anybody that you are upset or angry with?"

Like a lightbulb, her expression brightened immediately, followed by a dissolution into tears of relief. Thus began her story.

Maria was a Hispanic mother of two young children and a stay-at-home mom. She had looked forward with great anticipation to a visit from her sister, who lived in Mexico. She was coming to visit Maria and her mother, who lived just a few blocks away. Maria had bent over backward fixing up the guest room and planning a menu to celebrate their reunion.

As it turned out, Maria's sister spent the entire week at their mother's home and had not acknowledged Maria's preparation efforts. She had not even bothered to come and see Maria's house.

Like icing on a bad cake, her husband of eleven years had forgotten her birthday as did the visiting sister from Mexico. Guess what? Instead of confronting the thoughtlessness of her husband and the cavalier attitude of her sister, Maria decided to suffer in silence. She had not said a word to either of them about the matter.

Trouble was, her body was not so willing to remain silent in the affair. She certainly admitted to having attack thoughts and was not just a little proud that she had not acknowledged her husband's and sister's callousness.

After getting the above "off her chest," she said she felt much better and promised to make amends when she got home.

Her lab work was all normal, all $300 worth, and to my knowledge, her symptoms disappeared and have not recurred.

Left unresolved, do I believe Maria's case could easily have evolved into a more chronic one? Absolutely. Sooner or later, the poison of unforgiveness will work its way through the neutral body's system until there are objective measurable lab abnormalities and objective, physical manifestations of incorrect thinking. Depending on the circumstances, the doctors would ultimately be able to label it as something and it would be treated with an increasingly complex regimen of medications to interfere with the neutral body's response to commands it receives to attack. The lesson learned here: *When you attack, you attack yourself.*

Ron and Rheumatoid Interrupted

Ron's case is an example of how anger suppressed over a long period of time can surface and wreak havoc many years later. It also shows that with acknowledgment of the battle and desire to learn to see things differently, you can get better and perhaps discontinue medications you thought you were condemned to take for life.

Ron's case presented in a most unusual way, but with the advantage of hindsight, a problem was going to surface one way or another.

On a trip with his spouse hiking the Arches National Monument in Utah, Ron ran into problems. The group he was with got ahead of him. Being competitive all his life, but not wanting to admit it, he became angry as he pushed harder to catch up. As they were a long way from base and not wanting to slow the rest of the group, he pushed on, ignoring the pain that was building in the calf of his leg. By the time he arrived at his car, he was miserable. The next day as he walked the corridors of the Denver, Colorado, airport terminal, his leg throbbed and he was limping.

Arriving home, he came to see me and within a few days it became apparent he had mononeuritis multiplex involving the peroneal nerve of his leg. I use the fancy name to reinforce the idea we physicians like to put a name on things.

As it turns out, there are a number of causes for this condition, including several autoimmune diseases. In Ron's case a positive rheumatoid factor and elevated sedimentation rate confirmed the diagnosis of rheumatoid arthritis with associated inflammation of the blood vessels supplying blood to the nerve in his calf. I referred him to a specialist for further confirmation and treatment. That was certainly standard care at the time.

Having been started on his medication, which initially included small doses of steroids, he returned to me for followup. That's where looking at his past habits of behavior could help Ron in the here and now.

I had known Ron for a long time and was aware he had issues with anger even as a teenager. He was a rebellious child and had prided himself on his independence at an early age, particularly from his father. He made his own spending money and resented any financial help. He also felt that he was never good enough in his father's eyes. Ron liked playing linebacker in football and frequently would purposely make himself mad by visualizing the opponent doing something to his mother. He was not just a little proud of his ability to turn his anger off and on at will, or so he thought. Ron, over the years, cultivated his anger like a well-tended East Texas garden.

His joint symptoms remained relatively mild until his retirement from one of the service industries and he began to come into more contact with his father. By his own admission, he had a love/hate relationship with him. He found himself looking for opportunities to point out his father's unappreciativeness when the father did not note Ron's efforts to help his father around the farm. He did not tell his father or confront him. He just chose to stew about it. He liked playing the role of the victim. Ron was activating old tapes of anger that had started in childhood. He expected the future to look like the past. It was clear that Ron had become comfortable with his anger. He thought that it was what had made him an all-star football player in high school and was almost perversely proud of it. It made him feel more like a man. He could not see the fearful little boy of his childhood behind his manly facade he insisted on maintaining.

Over the next couple of years, his symptoms were moderately

well controlled with his medicines until the pain in his "good leg" got his attention. This threatened his independence enough that he became willing to consider that there might be a better way. Sometimes, you need to get hit on the head with a hammer more than once to wake up.

I taught Ron to start practicing a new idea. I kept it simple. Each time he encountered somebody, anybody, whether he was aware of his attack thoughts or not, to stop and say quietly in his mind, "Be kind, for everyone you meet is fighting a great battle." That was it. Stop and repeat the phrase. It did not matter if he were going to talk or have an interaction with the person. Even if he were watching a live news program. Remember: *Be kind for everyone you meet is fighting a great battle.*

I did put him on a low-fat diet and he finally started doing some cardiovascular exercise. Slowly, with the help of his lovely wife and some inspirational friends, Ron began to soften. He smiled more because he was less angry as the truth of Philo's admonition dawned upon him. He stopped seeing the world as his enemy but, instead, gradually became the world's friend.

Not surprisingly, his joint pain improved and he was gradually able to wean himself off his medications.

With Ron, it may take a long time to develop a forgiving heart. He has been playing those anger tapes for much of his life. But for now, it appears that the process of self-attack has been interrupted. Fortunately, it occurred before the much more expensive and potentially hazardous treatments had become necessary to try and put out the fire.

Sometimes you live with a problem so long it becomes a possession and the thought of giving up the illness produces so much anxiety and depression, it seems best to leave things alone. That is the situation with June, whom I use to point out that conditional forgiveness is no better than no forgiveness at all.

131

June and the Case of Deferred Adjudication

I met June many years ago when I started my practice in the late seventies. She had four children and worked at the local chicken plant. She was referred to me because of a problem with painful swelling of the joints of her hands and feet which had gradually developed over the previous three months. Exam, X-rays and lab work confirmed the presence of rheumatoid arthritis and she began treatments with aspirin in adequate doses and gold shots which were considered to be standard care at the time. After many months of treatments, her joints settled down and she went into remission by all objective measures.

She did, however, continue to have pain. The pain was always there, but for a long time it was not incapacitating enough to keep her from working at the plant. Raising her four children took all the money she and her husband could muster. Both had blue-collar jobs and money issues were always present.

Since I saw her frequently, June became more comfortable around me and shared more and more information about her personal life.

It seems that shortly before the onset of her joint symptoms, June discovered her husband was having an affair with another woman. Although she considered leaving him, close consideration of the effects of divorce on the kids and the economic realities of trying to raise the four children on her wages pushed her to stick it out. She was not happy about it, to say the least. Even back then, I could see how June felt trapped and I felt sorry for her as I put myself in her shoes. The best advice I could offer at the time was, "Let go and let God." Those trite words in my spiritual infancy still ring hollow today as I am forced to remember them.

June, a confessing Christian, assured me she had forgiven her husband of breaking the marital vows, but she told me she just could not forget it. And for the next twenty-five years, she held this indiscretion over her husband's head like a meat cleaver. In the entire time I knew June (she, along with her long suffering husband, have since moved away), I do not recall her ever having a kind word to say about him. June's idea of forgiveness is actually quite common. Perhaps the way most people think of forgiveness is really deferred adjudication.

Deferred Adjudication

This is a legal process and I think it is an excellent way to deal with mistakes in the law, but, is an ineffective way to deal with problems mentally. Legally, it says to the accused party, we are going to put this issue aside and not make a legal decision about your guilt; we are going to watch and see how you do over a period of time. If you keep your nose clean, so to speak, we will drop the charges. If you mess up, we will nail you for the new offense and prosecute you for the old one as well.

Mentally, most people do not let go and let God. Instead they push the offense below their conscious mind and secretly give permission to God to get the offender and punish him like he deserves.

That kind of "forgiveness" just pushes the anger and fear below the conscious perception of it. The biological effect goes on unabated, frequently turning up here or there, depending on the physiologic conditions and genetic predispositions as this disease or that and the long suffering continues.

June taught me there are many people who are attached to their misery. It is a possession. It confirms in their mind what a lousy world this is. Things would have been so different if he or she had not done that to me. It is the world's fault I am sick and it needs to fix me.

Over the years, I have learned through grace that the "yes, but" response is a warning sign telling me to take my attempts at communicating my idea for forgiveness as true pardon, and try it on someone else for now.

People like June seem to enjoy holding others entrapped with *guilt,* not recognizing they have shut the door of freedom on themselves as well. Their refusal to give up their right to judgment, by putting the apple back on the tree, is simply less frightening than taking another path.

The late Marlon Brando once said, "Guilt is a useless emotion; what we need is a healthy sense of conscience." The older I get, the more I find myself agreeing with this famous actor's "observation". I believe hanging on to guilt can be an insidious form of spiritual pride. The emotion can definitely make you physically sick as we will see in the next chapter.

Chapter 9

Guilt and Illness

Can one become a saint without God? That is the only concrete problem I know of today.

Albert Camus

The more sinful and guilty a person tends to feel, the less chance there is that he will be a happy, healthy or law-abiding citizen. He will become a compulsive wrong-doer.

Dr. Albert Ellis (American psychotherapist)

I did not come to call the righteous, but sinners.

Jesus in Matthew 9:13

I think the story of Adam and Eve in the Garden should be required reading for all first-year medical students. Then, after the first-year internship, it should be required again. Every five years when the physician renews his or her medical license, it should be required once more.

This wonderful mythical story really does have profound lessons for those who take the Hippocratic oath. It also has profound lessons for those who go to consult them.

Sometime, somewhere in the distant past, the idea of a right behavior and a wrong behavior entered the mind of our early ancestors. I do not know if that was in ancient Mesopotamia, as some maintain, or deep in Africa as others assert. But somewhere and for some reason, that first Adam felt the painful feeling of self-reproach and for many it has been Hell ever since. Whoever He and She were, they can be congratulated for ultimately running up the medical bills for millions and millions of people, even today.

You can look at a large part of the two trillion dollars that America spends on sick care each year as a continuing payment for that first bite of the apple that led to the delusion that we could judge for ourselves without escaping judgment. That was one expensive apple. Guilt is an expensive emotion.

We are going to consider briefly the biology of punishment, and the origin of the different sets of laws. Finally, I will share with you how guilt plays itself out in medical practice by examining the widespread problem of obesity and the rare problem of the "red man syndrome". I will also show you how the Bible can be used to discourage rather than encourage - how it can be used to promote guilt.

I think most, if not all of us, have experienced this emotion, but I believe we should stop and define the term guilt.

Guilt: *a painful feeling of self-reproach resulting from a belief that one has done something wrong or immoral.*

Webster's Dictionary

Lower animal studies have not revealed a "guilt" center in the limbic area of the brain. I do think we need to review the biology of the fear and punishment center to better understand guilt. I think guilt may be one of those emotions we have chosen to indulge ourselves in, to allow us to separate ourselves from our brother animals. I think it is more a frontal lobe phenomenon. Having said that, I will contradict myself below when we consider the three sets of laws.

Biology of Punishment

We have discussed the biology of fear and anger by looking at studies of the brain involving our monkey cousins and have come away with some rather interesting observations regarding our own human brain. There are areas of the brain that, when stimulated, cause the animal to show signs of discomfort and restlessness. Continue with the electrical signals, and these signs progress to fear and pain, eventually leading to illness. If you continue to stimulate these centers, the animal will gradually cease to eat and drink and will eventually die. This is called the fear/punishment center. We discussed this area of the brain in Chapter 4.

Remember, if you stimulate the reward and pleasure centers of an animal and allow him control over that stimulus he will pour on the juice. However, if you take over the role as the stimulator and increase the intensity, the animal will eventually display anger and rage. It is though the animal says: Enough is enough. If left on his own, he knows when to stop before the anger and rage stage.

Now let us take it a step further. Let us stimulate the reward/pleasure center and simultaneously stimulate the punishment/fear center. Guess what happens? Punishment and fear win out and the animal will display the rage and/or withering sickness response.

In summary, biological studies of the brain show that punishment and fear win out over pleasure and reward in animals.

Now how about you and me? I think even if you only have a casual interest in examining your own behavior, you will conclude that the same applies to you.

Psychologists have believed for a number of years that human behavior can best be understood as an attempt by each of us to maximize our pleasure and avoid pain or discomfort. Among others, we have Dr. Sigmund Freud to thank for this observation, and from a strict biological standpoint, I think he was correct. That we are programmed to behave that way is and has been taken as a matter of faith, no pun intended. What the experiments of animal models above would seem to indicate is that ultimately it is not a zero sum game. Fear and punishment win out in terms of observed behavior. In other words, in our attempt to maximize pleasure, we will   participate in more and more destructive behavior, thus leading to our own demise where fear and punishment reign. Now who do you think is laughing at this predicament in which biological man finds himself? If you said the devil or ego, go to the head of the class. Remember, in the studies of the monkey I noted above, if you let the animal pour the juice to himself, he enjoys it but "knows" when to stop most of the time. But if an outside force takes control, all havoc is wrought.

That "outside" experimenter or controller in your own case is the devil or ego. I have told you before that I personally prefer the term devil because it acknowledges how powerful your adversary is in the battle for your allegiance.

Guilt and Human Behavior

Now let us take this mental self-examination a step further. We do not know if any other animals experience the painful feeling of guilt, but simple examination of our own thoughts and memories would indicate that most, but not all, Homo sapiens have at one time or another experienced the uncomfortable sensation of self-reproach. In my own case, the feeling of guilt is felt in the center of my chest, in the general area of my heart.

Like most adages, "my heart's not right" contains some powerful truth, not the least of which is physiologic. We may use this saying when we have done something "wrong," using some measuring stick for judging our own behavior.

Some people might say the pang of guilt I feel in my heart is a result of the frontal lobes of my brain being so programmed by my early childhood training that the fear and punishment caused the release of stress hormones that in turn produced some sort of physical discomfort. To a point, I would agree with my scientist friends, but there may be more going on here than can be measured and observed.

Personal experience has convinced me that my mind, which is part of "The Mind" is not confined to the brain but shares a common communication center, that being the organ, the heart.

When the Lord said in Jeremiah 31:33, "I will put My law in their minds and write it on their hearts," He did just that and He still does. I believe you have to be born again in order to receive the blessing of this recognition. The Guide that you receive when you acknowledge the atonement of Christ will gradually and lovingly shift the center of your outward behavior from your brain to that much warmer and kinder organ, your heart. He will teach you to think with your heart rather than that much over-rated, cold and calculating brain.

Three Sets of Laws

Biological Law   **Laws of Man**   **The Great Law**

Man has three sets of laws that can govern his behavior. First, you have the biological laws that are roughly the same laws that govern the behavior of the animal world. I have described these laws earlier and, as I not so delicately put it, you are either *dinner or diner* when these laws are operative. I remember very clearly an epiphany I had in 1990 regarding this.

I had recently read Desmond Morris's *The Naked Ape.* The gist of the book is that modern man descended from or ascended from blood-thirsty killer apes. Notice the "descend" or "ascend" depends on the direction you think evolution is traveling. It was late in the evening and I had been reading the Bible and reflecting on those "crazy" words that Jesus had said in my favorite gospel of John. He said in John 6:53: "Truly, truly, I say to you, unless you eat the flesh of the Son of Man and drink his blood , you have no life in you." All of a sudden, I realized this man Jesus knew exactly the nature of man's nature. The thin veneer of civilization of the Roman empire had masked what we truly are without God. He knew that Homo sapiens man was a fighting, eating, sex machine that I referred to earlier. He was driven by a set of laws that included the possibility of cannibalism. He knew us as we really are without supernatural help. His own sacrifice of actual blood would be the only thing that would resonate with the truth of where our flesh came from. It was the only thing that would satisfy man's underlying bloodlust. He was the perfect answer to the collective guilt that we carried within us.

If you were going to make up a way to atone for the guilt that accompanied blood-thirsty behavior, Jesus was the perfect answer. Yet the historicity of the life of Jesus was and is as well-documented as any event we hold to be true in our recorded history.

The same night as my "epiphany", I recalled what my seer, my retired minister friend, had told me 12 years earlier. "Joe, don't go to Jesus until you can accept him intellectually." That was the night I recognized His story was indeed the greatest true story ever told. Let me also add that accepting Him intellectually is not the same as surrendering to Him. That would take another twelve years in my case.

Laws of Man

The second set of laws that govern man work through the frontal lobes of the brain. As Homo sapiens evolved as a larger, more numerous social species, they developed an impressive set of frontal lobes within the brain. The frontal cortex allowed the "be fruitful and multiply" command to take place in at least a more "civilized" manner. We covered ourselves and laid down our spears and hatchets frequently enough to allow us as a species to develop agriculture, cities, art and laws. The frontal lobes took on more function as we grew more numerous and crowded. They helped to keep our more bestial appetites of sex, eating, drinking, and fighting in check. At that point, life, as it was known, was both short numerically and filled with pain. History does not record that there was any great demand for psychiatric couches and/or medication for the emotion guilt.

I believe the emotion guilt made its widespread debut with the appearance of written and oral laws. The Ten Commandments certainly appear to be a reasonable place to start if you are trying to run rough-shod over a bunch of whining, ungrateful, barely civilized former slaves. Mosaic law tried to pull man's attention away from the more primitive laws of his biology as noted above. The frontal lobes of the brain were where the first laws were taken in and, with a few centuries of practice, allowed us to do the harder thing of keeping our bestial drives somewhat in check. Then more laws were added and the burden of following them grew as did the sense of failure when we broke them. Guilty emotions evolved particularly in the lives of those at the bottom of the food chain.

Backbreaking work, fifty percent childhood mortality rate, an average life expectancy of twenty-eight years, brutal overseers and rapacious tax collectors were the order of the day two thousand years ago. And that was in the setting of the most technologically advanced society of the day, the Roman Empire.

The sinners at the bottom sought a little temporary pleasure in that ghastly world they were living in. It was asking too much of the do-the-harder-thing frontal lobes. Lapses in behavior occurred frequently as the bestial desires got the best of them, and those written laws were violated more frequently. Failure to behave appeared to be inevitable for at least some.

The rulers and priests of those days reinforced these feelings of guilt of the common man as they accepted the sacrifices of meat and grain offerings as an atonement for the inability to keep at least the outward behavior in line with the laws, these brain laws. Guilt, as well as our identification with the body, grew as the cycle of failure to keep the laws simply led to more sacrifices. This reinforced the fear of a punishment from the powerful, unapproachable, capricious Creator. Like their pagan brothers, the Israelites projected onto God the very same qualities they saw in themselves and others. The educated priestly class, being blind themselves, continued to lead their charges down a guilt-strewn path. The priests reinforced the lie that you are your body and you are separate from God. This simply confirmed what their physical perceptions were telling them: *This is a dog- eat-dog world and true danger lies just around the corner.* No wonder their life expectancy was only twenty-eight years.

The Great Law

Finally, Jesus appears on the scene and establishes up front that He came to redeem and not condemn. His central teaching can be summed up, I believe, in the Golden Rule. Many people confuse this as one more law like the Ten Commandments. "Do to others as you would have them do to you." It is not. It is a statement of fact. "As you do unto others it will be done to you." He even extended it to your thinking. He knew that if your thinking was perfect, your behavior would be perfect and you would be happy. That law, the Great Law, is written on your heart. The part of your mind that is in your heart understands this Golden Rule.

Down very deep in your heart, you know your reality. Your reality does not have to be a continual cycle of trying to obey the brain laws and then breaking those laws as your lower nature or biology kicks in. You can be governed by the Spirit where there is no guilt. You can and will make mistakes while you inhabit this physical body, but the destructive emotion of guilt can be given back to the devil, its author, once and for all.

How? You may ask. By receiving His forgiveness, you are charged to live by the Great Law: Forgive and you will be forgiven.

Jesus and the Laws

We have discussed the various ways guilt can arise from looking at the three sets of laws that can govern our behavior. One of the things that has always puzzled me was the question of why Jesus did not write down His teachings. Was He just being kind to the future biblical commentary business?

Below are some of my tentative conclusions:

First, the problem of the tower of Babel. There was not a universally spoken language 2000 years ago. His message is for all of us. Not just for those who can read, not just for those who can hear. Jesus was said to have spoken Aramaic, the most common oral language in the Levant 2000 years ago. Therefore, what we have as written text today are translations and shall remain just that, translations.

Second, to write His words down would lead us further into trusting our views of this perceptual world. I think in some strange way it would have added to our worldliness. Sometimes the written word hinders "seeing" with our spiritual eye.

Third, I think He wanted to communicate with all men in a way like no other. In a way, that makes the Internet, texting, and cell phones seem like child's play. He was going to send the Guide, the Holy Spirit, that would leave no doubt about its supernatural origin once you experienced it. You would be left with the absolute certainty that your little view of reality and its means of communication are laughably restricted. Each of us has our own symbols and cues. The Holy Spirit will use those in getting the Master's teaching across.

In summary, I think Jesus did not write His teachings down because He knew there would be the self-righteous of this world who would wave the writings around and stir up guilt and tell people what to do. He wanted to come to you directly and wake you up from this very bad dream gently using the symbols that are special to you. It was part of His plan for a personal relationship with each of us.

Modern Day Guilt

Is the feeling of guilt still present today and does it have a role in medical illnesses? The answer is a resounding " yes," certainly from the perspective of my clinical practice. Moreover, with my own identification with the physical body and projection of my fears onto my patients, I contributed to the emotion greatly. Remember Larry of the pizza dinner story? Each time I browbeat him with regard to the laws of nutrition, I wanted him to feel guilty that he was not doing what I told him to do. Like the priests of old, I was laying down one more set of laws regarding what was clean and unclean concerning his dietary habits. In short, I was adding to his burden of guilt as I reinforced his idea in a set of laws that were totally arbitrary and had no chance of fixing his problem. It is not that the rules of nutrition were a heavy burden for him, but it did just add to his pile. I did reinforce his own identification with his body as the answer to who he was.

The Bible Used As a Guilt Weapon

As I stated earlier, I consider myself a born-again Christian. The whole process of being born again is to give you new vision. Literally, you do not see things as before. The change in my own vision has been quite startling.

The Sunday newspaper has a section where you are supposed to find a hidden object in the picture. You stare and stare and finally you see it and say to yourself: How could I have missed it? It was there all along. It is really a very common reaction among born-again Christians. The training manual for the Christian is the Bible, and not unlike that newspaper and its hidden objects, the wonderful and profound truths were there all along. It required the "new vision" to see them.

Problems arise when we assume our individual view of this newfound truth is the only way to see it, since this tends to lead to self-righteousness. The danger multiplies when we get a group who, at least temporarily, agrees that this is for sure the truth. The "new vision" becomes cloudy as sects, denominations, and divisions within lead to a further separation from our brothers and sisters.

The history of organized religion has its share of problems, many of which can be traced to the worship of the Bible rather than its central figure, Christ. It has been interesting to note in my medical practice that some of my patients who have had the most problems with high blood pressure and anger issues are those "born again" Christians. Some have the tendency to use the Bible as a knife in dividing up who gets into heaven and who does not. They try to use guilt to manipulate others into agreeing with them.

Bible-Thumping Earl

I met Earl relatively early in my career, long before I became born again. From the beginning, I really did not like Earl. He was loud and aggressive and always seemed a little angry. Very early on in our first meeting, he let me know he was a Christian and he knew his Bible. Over the twenty-year span he came to my office, I cannot recall a single time he did not quote scripture, giving me chapter and verse just to make sure I knew how good his memory was. He was a faithful tither and was fascinated by my least-favorite book in the Bible, Revelation.

Almost every time Earl would leave my office, I had this lingering feeling that Earl wanted me to feel guilty if I did not agree with his interpretation of a particular scripture. Over the years, I learned never to question him on the exact words found in the King James Version, because he was invariably right. He was as impressive a lay biblical scholar as I have ever encountered.

However, one of the most troubling quirks that actually made me cringe was the almost perverse way he relished final judgment. He seemed to enjoy the idea that some of his fellow human beings were going to be left out of heaven if they did not espouse his view of things. It seemed he took perverse pleasure in the idea of those sinners burning in hell forever.

Like most of us, he picked those things in the Bible that agreed with his own personal preferences and, as a literalist, Earl saw the Bible to mean what Earl said it meant, literally. Unfortunately, his behavior turned me off as it apparently did others. He had very few friends. As I said, he was always angry about something. It was no wonder he came to me for high blood pressure. He was also 35 pounds overweight and had an elevated cholesterol. Ghandi once said, "I like that man Jesus, it's the Christians I have trouble with." I suspect Mr. Ghandi had met somebody like Bible-thumping Earl.

In dealing with Earl's problems, diet and exercise were no more effective than you might imagine. Earl was always too busy to commit to anything that required taking time out or slowing down. He had a number of business interests and was quite successful financially. If he wasn't busy at his store, church activities always awaited. His blood pressure seemed to follow his level of frustration at others who got in the way of his plans. He was always angry at this city official or that banker or politicians up in Washington who were "running this country into the ground." Welfare recipients were one of his favorite targets of ire.

I tell my friends you will frequently have to go through a lot of Christians to get to Christianity.

If Earl had been my only contact with Christians in my life, I would have run the other way. If this is what reading the Bible can do, no thanks. Fortunately, Earl's behavior is not representative of most Christians. I have included him as an example of the hazards of using guilt as an effective tool in bringing others around to your point of view. I also use it as a warning against the idea that reading the Bible will get you into heaven. It will not.

There was nothing about Earl's behavior (his fruit) that indicated he had the "peace that passes all understanding." His constant fretting over church and business activities was a long way from the simple life of quiet and trust the Guide provides even in the midst of all our pursuits.

Obesity and Guilt

Morbid obesity is a puzzling phenomenon. In fact, it is one of the most interesting problems I have dealt with in medicine. Recently, it received the coveted definition of an official disease, thus freeing it up for insurance reimbursement in the treatment thereof.

The estimate is that 65% of Americans are overweight as defined by a BMI (body mass index) of greater than 25. We have 30% who fall into the category of obesity with a BMI of over 30. I include these numbers to confirm science's addiction to measurement, to objectify the issue. It is as if classifying it and putting numbers on it brings it closer to being understood which, as has been noted before, is a fundamental error.

Most fascinating is the phenomenon of morbid obesity, defined as a BMI of greater than 40. In America today we have approximately 3 million bodies in excess of 300 pounds, and 400,000 bodies that weigh more than 400 pounds - the latter being mostly males.

The reason for the term "morbidly obese," is that there appears to be an apparent risk of early death from heart disease, stroke, and diabetes in people who are greater than one hundred pounds over their ideal body weight. That is, they have an increased mortality compared to the normal weight individual.

My interest in preventive medicine and the "laws of nutrition and exercise" that I espoused led me to encounter more of these individuals than the average internal medicine doctor. In my thirty-odd years of dealing with this issue, I have these observations to make:

#1. Guilt in treating this problem does not work. Our morbidly obese brothers and sisters cannot be shamed into following some set of rules of behavior. Dr. Albert Ellis accurately pointed out the more sinful and guilty a person tends to feel, the less chance there is that he will be happy and healthy. He will become a compulsive wrong-doer. I tried shame and guilt at various times trying to help, and it only made the problem worse. Fear only increases the compulsion to eat, and we know guilt and fear go hand in hand.

#2. Through the use of diet and exercise alone, I, personally, have not been successful one single time in seeing a patient lose their excess weight and keep it off for two years. Not one single time that I am aware of. A simple mechanical solution does not work. I think there is a profound lesson in looking at this problem. I do not believe it is all genetics.

#3. The fat and jolly moniker is a lie. The morbidly obese are, in general, as unhappy and depressed as the general population, perhaps more so since their sense of not being able to help themselves adds to their frustration.

#4. Rarely did the morbidly obese come to see me because of the obesity itself. Physical appearance was not the primary concern. It was usually due to the pain or discomfort of a co-morbid condition such as degenerative arthritis of the knees or inability to breathe due to asthma or congestive heart failure.

#5. Almost invariably, the morbidly obese patient was brought in by a family member, friend or loved one. They did not come in of their own free will. They obviously and correctly sensed that the traditional idea of diet and exercise was not going to help them. In general, they are the masters of the "yes, but" excuse of why they cannot follow a program. Just as in June's case in the previous chapter, it became clear that without the supernatural help of the Guide, I could only help their symptoms. I could not fix their problem. Also, as in June's case, with her joints, my focusing on the weight issue of the obese only served to confirm a body identification which was playing right into the ego's insane beliefs, both the patient's and mine. I allowed myself to focus on the seen rather than the unseen.

#6. The morbidly obese almost always have a co-conspirator. Just as in the case of the alcoholic, there is usually an enabler, like a mother, father, wife or girlfriend who supplies the ammunition for the self-attack. This is usually done with the outward face of "caring" which covers the perhaps murderous attack the enabler wishes to hide.

#7. I believe most of us secretly like having the morbidly obese around. It supports our natural tendency to be judging machines. We smugly want to exclude these individuals from our circle of holiness. They conveniently give us somebody to compare ourselves to as we arrange the totally delusional ideas of a hierarchy of "sins" in our own minds.

#8. I do not believe obesity is a disease, but it is a very visible confirmation that we are all fighting a great battle. The morbidly obese represent as good a place as any to work on putting the apple of judgment back on the tree. They represent one end of the spectrum of body identification of which each of us on Planet Earth must rid ourselves if we are to be happy, healthy, free and fearless.

#9. As radical as it may sound, the overeating that accompanies morbid obesity, as in the case of all self-destructive behaviors, is an attempt to make the world look better for a while, then not. It is one more attempt doomed to failure as we use the body as anything other than a neutral means of communication. It is the result of the idea that you can destroy yourself, who you are. It is just an attempt at suicide with a much slower trigger.

Remember the case of Therese Neuman. I was just as mistaken as most when I was so sure the "laws" of nutrition were set in stone. Apparently not. I have been a well-intentioned do-gooder for most of my medical career.

#10. I confess I treated obesity rather simplistically for a long time. There might be something deeper going on here involving issues of which we are unaware.

I have this to say to the morbidly obese: You are a guiltless child of God, forever safe, having everything. You are spirit, you are not your body, and I apologize and ask your forgiveness if I delayed your awakening to these truths. Just like the rest of us, you must begin each day admitting how lost you are and practice asking Him: Where am I supposed to go and what am I supposed to do? I guarantee if you ask these questions from the heart, He will answer you in your ordinary life here in this present moment. Remember, we are all in this fight together and you can choose to live in a guiltless, sinless world. It is up to you.

Tom, Guilt and the Red Man Syndrome

After my conversion experience, I began to see things differently. I mean very differently. If you had told me upon my graduation from medical school or during the first twenty plus years of practice that I would be approaching illness the way I do today, I would have said you had lost your mind. Actually, I lost my mind to the "new vision" that the Guide revealed and continues to reveal to me in my very ordinary, yet extraordinary, encounters.

As I noted earlier, I confess I may have observer bias. When your vision changes, your biases change. I do not see things as I once did.

In order to help the suffering and ill, I believe you must address spiritual issues head-on. If we want to be the best physicians for our brothers, we cannot ignore the thousand-pound elephant in the room by remaining aloof, obtaining only objective scientific data, and following some prescribed pathways of care.

I have been a faithful subscriber to the *New England Journal of Medicine* for thirty-seven years, beginning in 1972 upon graduation from medical school. It is certainly one of the most respected medical publications and is looked upon as the most relevant. Contributing authors are said to be some of the best and brightest of our colleagues in regard to the most up-to-date thinking and research.

Each week, there is an informative case presentation of some interesting disease process that unfolds like a Sherlock Holmes mystery. I enjoy entering into the role of the sleuth in uncovering the diagnosis by way of clinical discussion and later by confirmation from the pathologist. There is always an array of specially stained slides and increasingly complex lab analysis. If I do not read anything else, I read these cases. Since the change in my biases, I now find myself wanting to know more about the history of the described patients in these clinical vignettes. I cannot help but believe there are spiritual issues underlying many of the illnesses that are being missed.

The following case graphically illustrates how important a spiritual history is in trying to solve a seemingly unsolvable mystery.

I offer Tom's case not to indicate what a great sleuth I am, but in humble recognition of what a great teacher the Guide is.

Tom came to me a few years ago as a referral from a friend who said I knew something about rashes. That was a bit of an exaggeration. Tom had suffered from a nagging skin rash for about three years. It was more than nagging; it had become incapacitating. The symptoms of burning and itching of his skin were generalized. The condition interfered with both his sleep and work. He had sought consultations from the very best experts, including my old alma mater's Department of Dermatology, that branch of medicine that deals specifically with skin diseases. They prescribed steroids and gave his condition the label <u>Red man syndrome</u>, telling him it had something to do with his overactive immune system.

Feeling humbled by the credentials of the past experts, I resorted to what has always served me well in the past. I asked Tom about what was going on in his life when the problems with his skin started. Parenthetically, let me add that I inquired, as I nearly always do, as to Tom's religious beliefs.

He said he was a card-carrying Baptist, having been raised in the church, making his profession of faith at age eight or nine. Tom was, like many of us today, a remarried, once-divorced broken vessel. Just the sort of guy Jesus came to help. Tom had been divorced a few years before his skin problems began. At about the same time his symptoms started, he discovered that his former wife had been diagnosed with Huntington's disease, a progressive, degenerative genetic disease of the central nervous system. The disease ultimately led to her death as well as one of their three children who had also inherited the same disease.

Prompted by the Holy Spirit, I took a chance. I asked Tom the obvious question with the rather obvious answer: Do you feel guilty about leaving your wife and family?

"Guilty is not the word. It's more than that. I am angry. I blame myself for the way things turned out," Tom replied.

He was literally living in the outer darkness where the fire does not go out and there is weeping (he confided he had done plenty of that) and gnashing of the teeth (angry at himself).

What color do you think of when you think of anger? We see red when we get really hot. And if you do biopsies of the skin, inflammatory cells are found in large numbers. "Red man syndrome" was an appropriate, almost-perfect description of what Tom was suffering from. The use of steroids in Tom's case was to calm down the inflammation, to dampen down the body's "fires," so to speak.

"Tom, I think you are doing this to yourself. I think you are punishing yourself in order to beat God to the punch. God through Jesus and the message of the cross has declared you not guilty once and for all. God is not angry at you. His love is total and unconditional. If it were not so, all hope is just an illusion. His will is love, not punishment and condemnation. Accept His forgiveness for your mistakes and extend that received forgiveness to all you meet."

Happily, Tom did just that and he got well without the further need of steroids to do so.

I have included this story of Tom as an example of the old saying: Many things that can be measured don't count while some things that can't be measured do.

I would ask of you all, including my fellow physicians, that while you are about your measuring and prodding, at least consider the possibility that what is going on may have something to do with and is the result of something profoundly important that can't be measured.

I am not arguing for moral relativism (anything goes depending on the circumstances). There is plenty of that to go around. What I am saying is that guilt is a destructive emotion. God knew that, Jesus knew that. He did not and does not want that for His children's (which we all are) lives.

Guilt leads to fear and fear blocks the flow of love, which in the end is all there is. Guilt is a destructive emotion which leads to the idea you have something to defend. Christ's physical resurrection was the ultimate object lesson for us. It proclaims that we are not our bodies, we are Spirit and as our guilt keeps us identified with the body, we will continue in that "reality". "As a man thinks, so shall he be."

Most Christians would tell you what I have said is true. But they live like Tom, as if they had forgotten the implication of the identification with our resurrected Lord. The emotion guilt and the ensuing destruction of your neutral body keep you in chains. The only way <u>out</u> is to see everybody else as <u>guiltless,</u> including old Bible-thumping Earl. You can exclude no one from your circle of holiness. You can and will make mistakes which the Guide will help you to note and then quickly forgive. He wants to keep your attention in the present moment where Heaven is found while the ego or the devil wants you bound to the past which is hell, as Tom would be the first to tell you.

As we have seen in detail the physical implications of guilt, let us move on to the mental and psychological manifestations where the idea of God is frequently not seen to be enough: clinical depression.

Chapter 10

Depression:
A Case of Mistaken Identity

If there is a hell upon earth, it is to be found in a melancholy man's heart.

Robert Burton, 1621

And do not call anyone on earth father, for you have one Father, and he is in heaven.

Jesus, Matthew 23:9

Remember, this is a book about how to be happy and healthy. It is a book designed to point you in the direction away from victimhood. Do you recall Chad from the first chapter? You will remember how he blamed everything around him for why he was sick. One of his central complaints was about what a lousy father he had been given. He felt his father was partially to blame for why Chad was the way he was.

I recognized Chad's physical symptoms were related to "depression," but I elected not to reach for the prescription pad too quickly. At least one time, Chad needed to hear the truth concerning the prison door he kept closing on himself. I told Chad that he had forgotten who he belonged to; that he had misidentified his true Father. When he asked incredulously, "How do you know what I think?" I said Jesus told us, "By their fruits you shall know them." The fruits of Chad's true Father were missing, those of love, joy, peace, patience, kindness, goodness, faithfulness, self-control and generosity. Those are the fruits the Holy Spirit, the Guide, wants you to show.

The old saying that "a sad saint is a sad saint" might serve as an encouragement to my Christian brothers and sisters who find themselves chronically sad. That statement is saying: Wake up and remember to whom you belong. Wake up to your true identity.

Clinical depression is a major and growing problem in primary care medicine. It has no respect for age, sex or nationality. We in the United States spend more on it but that is largely due to the fact we have more money to spend. Unfortunately, more and more young people suffer from this as we see the decline in the family unit. People feel abandoned by those they feel they should trust the most.

Og Mandino's advice from *The Greatest Salesman in the World,* written in the scroll titled, "I will be master of my emotions," says "I will remain too busy to be sad." This remark has significant implications in our world today. With decreased physical activity both in children and adults, the incidence of depression, an extension of the sadness Mr. Mandino refers to, is on the rise. Technology, though fascinating and at times helpful, has led to a generation of fast fingers, visual acrobats and brain multi-tasking, but physically challenged couch potatoes.

The term "Prozac age" has been used to describe life in the past twenty to thirty years as more and more people of all ages join the flight to safety by using drugs to deal with this "meaningless" world. We blame the drug companies for the problem, somewhat perversely ignoring our own role in this increasing demand to ease the pain of our living.

Certainly, in my own practice, I have used and continue to use antidepressants, using the newer drugs which are a vast improvement over the old. They are, in fact, useful but I use them knowing full well they are a "Trojan horse" of sorts.

You can let the Trojan horse into your fort if you realize that it contains some enemies, most obviously the side effects of the medicines themselves. However, the horse also carries more subtle side effects you might not anticipate or choose to ignore. I believe antidepressants reinforce a reliance on something outside yourself to fix your problem. The improvement in mood that accompanies their use may lead you to put off until later some much-needed repair of poor thinking habits. Paradoxically, they can increase your fears of a scary world where your depression seems out of your control.

As I have indicated, I use antidepressants in helping my patients. Sometimes the severely depressed suffer from frank dementia or psychosis, and at that stage, platitudes about the power of positive thinking can be more about self-righteous cruelty than trying to help a lost brother. Even the use of electroshock therapy is sometimes necessary, and as odd as it may seem, is the only humane way to help someone out of a very deep hole. When someone is drowning, they need a life line, not swimming lessons.

All the practical principles for a forgiving vision are not easy. They are not quickly learned. Suffering is a fact of life in this visible world, and at times it calls for medications while we await the miracle produced by the changing of the mind. External interventions which include medications can help symptoms but ultimately do not fix the problem. However, sometimes helping with the symptoms has to be good enough.

I confess that I have let the Trojan horse of medications including antidepressants, anti-anxiety and sleeping aids, into my practice. I do believe the gifts offered are worth the effort of keeping an eye out for the enemies within.

Is It Really Depression ?

In our attempt to label all things, medicine, using the methods of description, we like to fit diseases into different groups. We do this with cancer, heart disease, diabetes and a whole host of other diseases as well. In labeling things, there is a certain amount of self-delusion that may have untoward consequences. We saw this in the use of statins to treat elevated cholesterol and in the use of certain medications to treat high blood pressure.

The unintended consequences are these: First, giving the patient a label implies an understanding of the disease, which is not true. The pathophysiology of various diseases is constantly being adjusted and reworked.

Second, it tends to depersonalize the encounter by labeling the person as a diagnosis rather than a real individual. Science may be able to record on a computer the following information: a thirty-eight-year-old white female with depression. But the true statement about her is: thirty-eight-year-old mother of three, recently separated from her husband, who cries herself to sleep at night.

The first may be easier to fit into a computer algorithm than the second but it results in the dehumanization of a real life problem. It also encourages the belief in a quick fix.

The benefits from the use of these accepted interventions usually represent the far end of the spectrum of any given condition. The naming and intervention as a cookie cutter approach is our attempt to make sense out of a rather disorderly and often chaotic picture. The deeper we look into a particular problem, the more questions arise to call into question the previous naming, grouping and intervening. This is true in all sciences including physics, chemistry and genetics.

It is a stated goal by some of the leading experts that in the not-too-distant future we will have genomic medicine. By examining your genes, we will be able to diagnose the problem before it arises, pick a product off the shelf and remedy what ails you.

There are those who believe that depression is largely a genetic defect. Indeed, there is a frequent familial basis for all mental disease. Although it is incredibly complex, there is the theory that given enough time and resources, science will be able to figure out what makes Sammy run and fix him. This sort of thinking is one of the enemies we let in when we use and allow the use of medications to "control" behavior. It is part of the Trojan horse.

These medications have a profound and powerful effect on the limbic system's pleasure and reward centers as well as the punishment and anger centers of the brain. These are not sugar pills, they are not a placebo. The effects are worthy of our careful consideration as we allow these agents into our neutral body's brain. They can mask your conscious awareness of fear but do not always suppress the physiologic subconscious effects on your immune system or your *fight-or-flight* system. Thus, the biological self-destruction that accompanies these responses can proceed unabated despite your not being consciously aware of them.

Severe depression is associated with a slowing down of all motor activity. Speech is slowed, pleasure/reward centers as well as pain/punishment are slowed. Motility of the gut is slowed and mental processing of information is slowed. The clinical picture is very similar to the hyperstimulation of the punishment/fear center discussed in the beginning of the last chapter. Just like the animal model, the person suffering from profound depression stops eating and drinking and will die if there is no intervention. It's as if they are punishing themselves.

When you treat these individuals, a paradoxical phenomenon may occur. As the profoundly depressed person begins to mobilize and have more energy, the incidence of suicide is more likely to occur.

For many years, it has been noted that this type of severe depression is frequently precipitated by anger directed inward. The individual feels so guilty about some misdeed, they literally execute the body. Suicide is a noted side effect in the use of antidepressants, particularly in the teen years, and now carries a "black box warning" of this potential outcome. Over the years, I have seen a few of the profoundly depressed in my practice and I find it striking just how many of them resembled the animal model described.

All this said, they represent only a very small number of people who carry the label of depression. The overwhelming number of prescriptions for antidepressants are written for what I call the "worried well." In our attempt to justify our use of these medications, we have reinforced the fears of a very large number of people. TV and magazine advertising now touts the use of these medications for a broad array of so-called problems as we try to medicalize life. It has advanced to the point that the viewer is told it may take more than one antidepressant to fix their unhappiness.

Zero Sum Game

Most physicians do not enjoy treating depression, at least according to the informal survey taken of my colleagues over the years. When I would see a depressed patient's name on my schedule, I cringed. At the time, they simply took too much out of me. They sucked out my vitality, my chi as the more hip would say. If I had more than two or three in a day, I was whooped, physically spent. It was as if I were engaged in a zero sum game. When they left, they always seemed better, at least temporarily, but I felt I had lost something. I was not really sure what it was but I used to say they sapped all my BTUs. I suspect that most physicians feel similarly.

In retrospect, I understand what was going on much better. In any encounter, there is the potential for the exchange of energy to occur. It occurs at a very primitive level, below the usual measurable standards. I believe that even though we are not aware of it we are constantly either giving or receiving love. The late Scott Peck, M.D., that wonderful ground-breaking psychiatrist, said that psychotherapy was, in fact, an act of love. Our attempts to help our brothers and sisters in our everyday, ordinary lives are the same psychotherapy and exchange of love on an unconscious level.

For the remainder of this chapter, I want to focus on what the authorities would call mild to moderate depression. Although the same principles apply to the severely depressed, they did not make up the bulk of the depressed patients that I encountered. What I came to understand through my new vision was my judgmental attitude. I learned I had to forgive these irksome patients before I could understand them, and through that forgiveness, I could now see them as my brothers and sisters and no longer as vitality-sapping leeches.

Early Treatment

Let us backtrack in the history of depression. It is certainly not a new phenomenon. Chronic unhappiness has been around for a long time. For many centuries it was known as melancholy. In medieval times, it was a state of mind thought to be caused by black bile, one of the four humors. The four cardinal humors thought to be responsible for your health and general disposition were blood, phlegm, yellow bile and black bile. The excess black bile caused gloominess, irritability and listlessness or tiredness. Like most diseases of the day, it was treated by barbers with bloodletting in an attempt to restore the balance of the four humors. The other mode of treatment for many ailments of that day was purging, whereby the person was given a concoction to make them either vomit or have diarrhea. Treatment options were, to say the least, limited, but even twelve hundred years ago we had our "descriptive scientists" at work trying to label and make sense of what was going on in their perceptual world.

Modern medicine can pat itself on the back for humanizing the treatment program of melancholy or depression. This has been of true value in the severely depressed. I am not so sure about all the others.

Recent studies have confirmed that exercise is just as effective as medications in the treatment of mild to moderate depression. "I will remain too busy to be sad" is not a bad way to start self-treatment. It was and is a valid way of a "fake it till you make it" approach until, or while, you are developing your new worldview. Physical movement helps to restore energy levels. The saying, "You must expend energy to get energy," is a very real physical fact.

Fatigue is a common symptom in this thing we call depression and, although it seems paradoxical, it remains true that you are fatigued because you are not physically active - not the other way around. Just as it is true that you are sad because you cry, not that you cry because you are sad. A frequent remark by my depressed patients is, "Doctor, I find myself crying for no reason." This means they have not yet arbitrarily assigned a reason for their crying. Remember Dr. Libet's experiment. Your physical act of crying precedes your awareness of your crying. The true you is always looking at the past. As with all of us, the past is a big problem for the melancholy, the chronically unhappy or the depressed.

Childhood and Depression

The one thing I can say about the depressed person from a family history standpoint is that they all have fathers and mothers. They may not have aunts or uncles, sisters or brothers, or biological children of their own, but they have parents. When I initially see a depressed patient, I do not know whether their mother and/or father are still living but I know that at one time they had a biological mother and father.

What I am getting at is that depression, chronic unhappiness, frequently has its onset in childhood, and the parent/child relationship is the most important one in determining your outlook on life. Obviously, it is not the only one, but it is the most important one when shaping your worldview.

I am absolutely convinced that is why "Honor your mother and father" is number five on the list of the Ten Commandments. The first four have to do with our relationship with God and the fifth our instruction regarding our relationship with our earthly parents. Notice the commandment does not say, "love your father and mother," "like your mother and father" or "obey your mother and father." It says "honor" them.

I believe the term honor carries with it the idea of not being born into this situation by accident. Your parents have some very important lessons to teach you. Odd as it may seem, you can learn lessons about what you do not want to do with your life as well as those you do from your experiences and relationship with your parents.

Let us face it, parents can do some pretty lousy things. They can even do some atrocious things. Unfortunately, they can at times do what most of us would call evil things. We can still learn and even honor the lessons learned from even those very evil things.

The Ozzie and Harriet mom and dad ideal does occur, but rarely.

The majority of parents just being so-so, neither really good nor really bad, are doing the best they can with what they have learned to work with.

It is simply staggering to me how many depressed, unhappy people still have problems with this relationship. I am not talking about just the depressed young people. I am talking about the middle-aged and the elderly still having "issues" with their mother/father. This is true whether the patient was an only child or one of several siblings. If you are an orphan from childhood, it certainly does not spare you from depression; it simply means you encounter different types of authority figures.

It is a well-known fact that most people's idea of God the Father is reflected in their experience with their own father. That can be a big problem. When Philo said, "Be kind, for everyone you meet is fighting a great battle," I think he would have said starting with your parents would be a good place to begin. Most often they were and are fighting the same battle you are and in truth are just as lost. Our father/mother were or are driven by their biology and they make selfish mistakes. Grievances are born as we play the "what if only" game. "If only this would have happened differently, then I would be happy." The whining goes on, the black bile rises and peevishness and irritability continue as unhappiness and depression set in. The depressed individual sees himself as unhappy due to some external event often related to a "mistake" by one or both parents.

Jesus said in essence that you should call no one on earth your father, for One is your Father and He is in heaven. But perhaps the person you should be able to trust the most has let you down and you figure God will too. A point of optimism before we meet Martha, a real life case of parent-blaming depression, is no matter how psychologically ill the child, parents are almost always worse. In a strange way, there is a general improvement in the mental health of the progeny when seen from the higher perspective.

Husband-Shopping Martha

I met Martha recently when she came to see me because of profound fatigue. She had sought care from a number of physicians over the last several years for a number of complaints, but headaches and fatigue were the most prominent.

She was an attractive, well-groomed, 32-year-old divorced lady currently living with her parents. She had experienced irregular menses for at least a decade and tentatively concluded her fatigue must be hormone-related.

She brought with her the latest results of her blood chemistries, including a thyroid profile. All the results were normal, but she thought that maybe there was simply something the other doctors had missed that I could measure.

At that initial visit, Martha pulled out her sack full of medicines she was taking, including three antidepressants, a sleeping pill and two medications for the treatment of migraines. She had been on the antidepressants for two years, and despite changing brands and dosages, she felt no better. Despite the regular use of the sleep aids, (both prescription and over-the-counter), she slept poorly.

Her social and family history were quite interesting as they hinted at a possible cause for her fatigue. She was raised, in my estimation, by attentive and caring parents. All three children had been home-schooled for most of their pre-teen and teen years. Two of the children had gone on to graduate from college. Martha's mother was a homemaker as well as the children's classroom teacher. Martha's father was an ordained Baptist minister and had faithfully served the church his entire working career.

Martha had made her profession of faith at age six and had been active in all church and youth group activities of her father's church.

Trouble started at home when Martha turned seventeen as she felt restricted by the rules around the house. She decided it was time to set out on her own. The following fifteen years proved to be turbulent, following a road of sexual promiscuity, recreational drug use and excessive alcohol consumption.

Remarkably, Martha graduated from college with a degree in business but had considerable difficulty holding down a job. For some reason, she always seemed to have conflicts with her boss. His fault, you understand.

Martha had been married three times, and when I saw her, she was dating a man ten years her senior who was separated from his wife although not divorced. Fortunately, none of her marriages had produced any children.

After getting a pretty good picture of Martha's life and before we proceeded to do hormone level testing, I asked, "Martha, is there somebody you are angry with, that you haven't forgiven for something?"

Almost before I could finish asking the question, she blurted out, "My father."

"Why is that, Martha?" I probed.

"He is so hypocritical. When I was growing up, all we ever had was rules, rules and more rules. If we made a mistake, we got spanked."

"Were you or your siblings ever injured?" I asked. When she shook her head, I proceeded. "What was the biggest reason for calling him hypocritical?"

"Doctor Davis, I heard my dad preach on love a million times, but at home I didn't feel loved. And when the newspaper would have something about some criminal activity, he would always say they ought to lock them up and throw away the key. Now I've met some people who have been in jail and I have to tell you, they don't seem that different from me. I mean I've done some things I'm not proud of, and if I would have been caught, I could have easily been in their shoes."

I was struck by the sincerity of this last observation and decided to go further.

"What do you call the overlooking of other's mistakes, Martha?"

"Forgiveness, I guess," she answered.

"Do you consider yourself to be a forgiving person, or are there people out there you think have done some things that remain beyond forgiveness? Is there something that irks you, that you have trouble forgiving?"

In the quietness that followed and as I looked into her eyes, I saw a light appear and then the tears began to flow.

"Martha, I have found that the first place to start when you are doing a forgiveness inventory are those closest to you. Forgiving in the abstract is really not all that hard.

"I have found most illnesses where unforgiveness plays a role involve close personal relationships and that most cases of depression involve an unforgiving heart. It usually starts with mother, father and siblings, but then spreads like a slow mental cancer. Fault-finding starts with those close personal relationships, then carries over to our marriages, co-workers, bosses, etc. Then we play the 'if only' game, if only I had a different set of parents, things would have been different.

"There comes a time when you have to stop that game and take responsibility for who you are and for your behavior. Your own hypocrisy is what makes you recognize your father's.

"When I say you have to take personal responsibility for who you are, I mean you have to establish once and for all the first of the three big questions: Who am I? Ultimately, it doesn't matter who I think you are. It doesn't matter who your father thinks you are. What does matter is you know who you are. And as long as you forget the new identity you received when you made your profession of faith of being a spirit child of God, you will physically suffer. Your mother and father may be responsible for the neutral body you inhabit, but they cannot give you the Spirit or Guide that can help you out of the mess you're in. That supernatural Spirit comes from above and you need to get back in touch with Him. I admit that being born again at age six, you may have a little trouble remembering, but He doesn't forget and He's waiting.

"The fact that you are physically tired when you get up in the morning indicates you are looking to the wrong source for energy. Your body is not telling you it is tired. Your mind is telling you that you are your body. This is the first error in your thinking you must correct.

"Tell me, Martha, do you ever feel good?" I asked.

"The only time I feel happy is when I am with my new boyfriend," she replied, leaving herself open for the rest of my sermonic bale of hay.

"Do you still read the Bible?"

"Occasionally at night," she said.

"Do you remember the story of the Samaritan woman at the well?"

"Vaguely," she replied. "I don't remember all the details."

"Growing up in a preacher's household doesn't guarantee a practical working knowledge of the Christian instruction manual. I suspect that what you think of the Bible will be colored by your current opinion of your father. Being the most widely read book in the world doesn't insure against misinterpretation of it. Martha, as Christians we don't worship a book; we worship Jesus Christ.

"It is very hard to understand how you can worship somebody you can't recall receiving something from and just maybe your idea of worshiping Christ is on the list of 'ought to' your dad taught you. I think your opinion of Jesus may be a rote exercise of recalling what somebody else taught you. I think it may be time for you to become acquainted with Him personally and find out what He is saying in your life, not what you think He's saying through your dad's life.

"As unfathomable as it may seem, God wants a very intimate and deeply personal relationship with you. He will reveal his presence in your ordinary life with all its errors and backsliding. The only place he can meet you is in the present moment. The only way that can happen is for you to make a sacrifice of your fears. The only way you can experience real energy, BTU energy that He can provide, is by looking to Him as the source. He is not jealous of your father or all your previous husbands. He just knew, even two thousand years ago, that you would grow tired of seeking completion where it cannot be found and turn to Him."

A Continuing Story

I do not know how Martha's story is going to end. Oh, I recognize the ultimate outcome in Martha's case is certain and it is a joyful outcome, even if Martha is not aware of it. She is Spirit, she is not her neutral body. Her preacher father is the origin of half of her body's DNA makeup, but she is not her genetic makeup. Those base pairs may determine her body shape and the color of her hair, even her courage or timidity. They may play a role in what foods she likes or dislikes, and in her attraction to the opposite sex. They may play a role in her tendency to be depressed, but they do not play a role in who she is beyond the workings of the five senses.

She is God's creation; she is Spirit as He is Spirit. She is love as He is love. Her energy can be limitless as His energy is limitless.

Over a few weeks' time, Martha and I visited about what

medicine had to offer her. We confirmed that her female hormones were in the normal range and, like the rest of the tests, did not indicate that her body was not ready to do what it was directed to do. I told her that the ancient wisdom of the body was telling her that emotionally she was not prepared to have a child, and rather than look at the irregular menses as a bad thing, perhaps her body was simply saying "not now".

We discussed the issue of divorce. She asked why I thought Jesus was so plain-spoken about the issue. I offered my opinion based on my bias since I, too, had been divorced. My own experience and confirmed by many of my patients is that divorce is one of the most painful mental experiences of life. Jesus knew that and did not want his friends to suffer. I believe we have to face up to the fact that we still have to use the tool of forgiveness wherever you go and whatever relationship you are in.

I think He wanted to spare us the wasted time of trying to find peace of mind and completion in biological relationships. It reinforces our identification with the body and its desires, thus delaying our ultimate satisfaction as we turn to Him. Each of us is whole in Him, but we act as if it is not so. How could He want that delusional thinking in our lives?

In our final visit, I told Martha what I had to offer her was my friendship. I assured her that I saw her true identity, but she might not agree. I told her I did not think the Trojan horse of medications was worth the dangers it contained as I pointed out to her the Guide that was available to get her out of the trap she thought she was in. I told her from now on she needed to look to her true Father as the lifeline, not medications, that what she needed now were swimming lessons. I told her she needed to learn about this man Jesus independent of what her father said. I suggested she start with that wonderful book by Emmet Fox, *The Sermon on the Mount.*

Healing of parent/child relationships with the understanding of the biology involved is crucial not only to the health of our brothers and sisters, but to society as a whole. As our parents age, the ever-increasing responsibility to care for them is falling on us, as it should, but we must learn to forgive their mistakes as we seek to be forgiven of ours and trust the Holy Spirit to guide us in honoring them.

What are we to do with our aging parents? What do we do to stem the rising phenomenon of dementia or Alzheimer's disease? What are we to do about a problem that threatens to crush our nation's economy and worsen the already overwhelmed medical system? Finally, what does forgiveness have to do with either one?

Chapter 11

Nursing Home Prevention Plan and Alzheimer's

An unused life is an early death.

Goethe in *Iphigenie auf Tauris*

Teach him to live a life rather than to avoid death. Life is not breath but action.

Jean Jacques Roseau

Therefore, however you want people to treat you, so treat them, for this is the Law and the Prophets.

Jesus in Matthew 7:12

By now it is clear that I believe that illness to a large measure is preventable. It is also apparent that the scientific methods used to describe and classify will soon lead to the rather broad decree that we are all ill in some manner. If you look deep enough, you will find some genetic mutation that will make patients of us all, and science will be able to enumerate for us what we are ailing from and fix it. All suffering will be named and a therapy assigned, whether it is a pill, regime, psychotherapy, vitamin program, hormone or genetic manipulation or tissue or organ transplant. If

175

that is not enough, cloning will ensure the perpetuation of something forever.

This picture is laughable. The problem is that there is a growing number of people, including scientists, who are buying into this delusion. It is not that they are not thinking, but they are thinking about the wrong things and this is where identification with the neutral body reaches its insane climax.

If you believe that life can be circumscribed and that this experience, your own existential experience, is all there is to life, you will be greedy enough to want to try and extend the experience for as long as you can. It is said that selfishness is the father of all sin. The attitude of focusing on the body is the ultimate selfishness. Meet sin in the twenty-first century. This is just the logical outgrowth of what Bob was trying to do in Chapter 7.

By sin, I mean separation from God. As I have said earlier, your reality cannot be separated from your Creator, but you can believe that you are separate from Him. This belief can temporarily have powerful effects on the world you live in.

If you believe in this separateness and the extension of the body's existence is all your life is supposed to be, you are working for the devil. At the center of this belief is something far more pernicious. It hides under the disguise of wanting to relieve suffering, where, in fact, it imprisons you to personal identification with the body. Fear of death draws you inexorably away from life and into the outer darkness where you deny your holiness.

Caring for the Elderly

Internal medicine implies caring for patients with medical as opposed to surgical problems. The training is separated after graduating from medical school as you move on to various hospitals for postgraduate medical instruction.

As I noted earlier, I did my internal medicine postgraduate training at Massachusetts General Hospital in Boston. The hospital is situated very close to the North End, a predominately Italian enclave of the city in the early 1970s.

What I learned in medical school, including the clinical rotations of the various specialities, had not prepared me for the first few months on the Bulfinch wards and the emergency room of that august institution.

I quickly realized there were few neat and tidy problems in medicine and those were usually confined to the very young. Instead, I realized that the actual practice of medicine took place amongst the elderly, chronically ill. Two-thirds of my time would be spent trying to help those over sixty-five.

A large number of the patients would arrive in the Emergency Room or on the wards. Their homes were usually one of the many nursing homes dotting the surrounding area. They would arrive with any number of common medical illnesses or a combination of medical and surgical problems. The vast majority of these illnesses were due to some rather predictable physiologic outworkings of a series of repetitive commonplace events.

Mamma Mia

Let us look at just one such encounter among the many that took place over a three-year period.

Mamma Mia was a 90-year-old lady of Italian heritage who presented to the Emergency Room of Mass General for the sixth time in the previous six months. She could provide no history because of her altered mental status. Review of the 12-pound medical chart was not encouraging concerning the prospect of

177

eventual communication. It seemed that Mamma Mia carried the diagnosis of OBS (organic brain syndrome) and had been in the incommunicado mode for the last seven years. In today's world and to be more politically correct, we would call it dementia or Alzheimer's disease.

It seems that Mamma Mia had been a good Catholic, and, along with Mr. Mia, had produced eight children. On this particular visit to the ER, they were nowhere to be found. A phone number of the oldest daughter was available, and as in most matriarchal societies she was the designated chief spokesperson.

When I called the daughter, it was clear that she had become emotionally detached from the scene. Since she had been down this road many times before, I could not really blame her. I brought the daughter up-to-date on her mother's current medical condition. Her mother was dehydrated, had aspiration pneumonia, and had a urinary tract infection from a chronic indwelling Foley catheter. The latter was placed to lighten the burden on the understaffed aides at the nursing home where Mamma Mia resided.

Though I was giving her daughter a current update, review of the old chart confirmed that this was a carbon copy of five of the last six admissions. In those days, we had a 72-hour overnight ward where we tried to work our miracle of snatching Mrs. Mia from the jaws of death. This included IV fluids, IV antibiotics, oxygen, frequent turning, and vigorous suctioning of her trachio-bronchial tree by the respiratory staff.

More often than not, we were able to accomplish this feat and deliver our charge back to her caretakers to see the whole process repeat itself again. The best I could hope for and see as a sign of humanity was the old lady's verbal responsiveness restored to an increasing cry of "mamma mia, mamma mia" That was it. It seemed that the brain's hard drive had been wiped out except for the last childlike cry of despair, "mother of mine".

As a matter of emotional survival, many physicians develop a seemingly thick skin in order to function in this kind of craziness. Others use black humor to cloud the futile vision that these cases can promote. My scientific education had not prepared me to deal with these social issues. Like a drowning man, I turned to the great wisdom literature for a life line. Central to my quest was coming to grips with death and people's fear of it.

In Mamma Mia's case, I was not afraid of her death. It was not my mother. If it were, I assured myself that I would not allow my mother to die in such an undignified manner.

Mamma Mia's daughter probably was not afraid of her mother's death either. She seemed to be somewhat indifferent. Perhaps because she had not come to grips with it regarding herself and could not recall how her mother felt about death, she and her family simply punted. They punted to the medical system to handle it, sort of. Although they claimed as a family they were ready for Mamma Mia to die, collectively they wanted to exert control over just how that physiologic process took place. As is often the case, they insisted they did not want her to die of thirst or starvation. They wanted me to give her IV fluids and feed her, if possible. They had bought into the myth that not eating or drinking must be painful and, with those "good intentions" projected their fears onto the medical system. And as was so often the case, they were not paying for these commodities of heroism. Somebody else was and, in this case, it was the Medicare and Medicaid programs.

The Myth of Starvation and Dehydration

This particular myth has caused a huge amount of grief and mischief. It insinuates itself into medical economics and is responsible for a very significant slice of total dollars spent on end-of-life care.

Homo sapiens are certainly interesting creatures, and as such, in dealing with this issue, I want to reemphasize the neutrality of the body when it comes to illness. Just as a child has a change in appetite over time, usually heading in an upward direction, aging is associated with a gradual decline in the same. The gradual loss of the senses of taste, smell and sight combined with decreased activity reduces caloric intake as the body winds down. Amid this decline is the decreased desire for food. The body does not tell the mind the desire is less. The mind desires less and directs these appropriate steps in the behavior. Remember Dr. Libet's experiment. Paradoxically, you experience the mental awareness for hunger because you eat, not the other way around. The ancient practice of fasting was designed to prove this point. It was and is an excellent way to prove who can be in control of the neutral body. Sister Therese Neuman's case represents an extreme example of the control over the neutral body's functions. She obviously was not tormented by hunger and thirst in thirty-five years of abstaining.

I have a friend who is Spirit-led who fasts for thirty days at a time with no sense of hunger and, interestingly, no measurable weight loss. Bobby says he feels quite well, even euphoric at times during his fast.

In the elderly, particularly those with dementia, thirst is not a problem. Physiologists have known for decades that the sense of thirst declines with age, and any discomfort actually is a result of a dry oral cavity which is easily remedied with a wet cloth or swab.

Ken's Good Death

It would be nice to disappear in the twinkling of an eye as it was said of Enoch of Genesis fame. However, sheer probabilities would suggest that the more prosaic will control the giving up of the body as a means of communication in most of our lives. I believe it is good thing for each of us to ponder the dissolution of the physical body, the neutral body. There is an ancient Zen Buddhist meditation where the pupil meditates on his own death, including the worms and maggots consuming the flesh. I have done this myself and it is actually quite freeing.

If you commit to using the body only for the sole purpose of communication, you will thwart the devil's or ego's desire to use it for pleasure, attack or show. When it is clear that it is no longer useful for the receiving and giving of love, then you will be able to set it aside fearlessly, as Ken's case demonstrates dramatically.

I had known Ken and Mittie for a number of years. They had both been patients of mine. Ken had a number of medical problems, including diabetes, high blood pressure, congestive heart failure and, ultimately, renal failure requiring dialysis. But metastatic kidney cancer is where this story begins.

Ken had been followed in Tyler, Texas, by the nephrology staff. Despite several unsuccessful attempts at dying, Ken hung onto the body, and its communication skills remained intact. Early one morning, Mittie called to remind me of my prior promise to be available to them until I went to their funeral or they came to mine. She felt that I could be of help and asked me to come. I went.

Upon entering Ken's room, I found a man struggling to breathe but still reasonably alert despite the large doses of medications he was receiving. After examining Ken and determining that without a miracle, Ken was very close to giving up the Spirit, or at least the body was close to its end of being a communication device. Ken was a devout Christian, which made the following conversation much easier for both of us.

Ken wanted to know if I thought he should take the chemotherapy the doctors were offering him. Despite the presence of lung metastasis, they said it might give him a few more months to live.

I told Ken that each man must make that decision for himself. I counseled him that if he could think of something he had not done, something that gave his life purpose, it would help signal the body that he was not through. After that, I recommended he take it one day at a time and focus on the "purpose".

As I always do, I asked Ken if there was somebody in his life that he was angry with or had not forgiven.

Both Mittie and Ken grew very quiet. Mittie was Ken's second wife and they had experienced a lovely marriage. He had a daughter from his first marriage whose name was Charlotte. Charlotte had been upset by Ken's divorce from her mother and had distanced herself emotionally from him. She had married some three years before and had asked her stepfather to give her away, to walk her down the aisle. Ken did not attend the wedding and had not spoken to her since.

I told Ken I now realized what God was expecting me to do. I was to deliver this message: Ken was to forgive his daughter immediately and not to put it off. He needed to call her as soon as possible and tell her he forgave her and to ask for her forgiveness. "But Ken, don't do it unless your heart is right," I said. What I should have said is, "Your heart won't be right until you do it."

Ken did not agree with my plan immediately. Instead, his last words other than thanking me for coming were, "Doc, I believe this is the outer darkness."

Less than twenty-four hours later, I received a call from Mittie, Ken's wife. It confirms how unfathomable God's grace is.

One hour after I left the hospital, Charlotte, his estranged daughter, called. Through the grapevine she heard her father was ill and asked if she could come. Mittie, almost speechless, managed a "Sure." She did not tell Ken.

Two hours later, the daughter walked into the room and the very first words out of Ken's mouth were, "I'm sorry, please forgive me." An hour later, Charlotte left, returning to her family in Dallas.

That night, Ken died. Mittie said it was a miracle. He closed his eyes after the last nurse's check at 11p.m. and his breathing stopped and he was gone. No struggle, no unfinished business, no one apparently left with whom he needed to communicate.

That's a good death and it is available to all of us if we just remember our purpose. The purpose is to be loving and forgiving until our last breath. Isn't that simple?

Purpose and the Prevention of Alzheimer's Disease

Alzheimer's disease is actually an anatomical diagnosis requiring brain tissue to make a definitive pathological diagnosis. The hallmark of the pathology of the brain is the presence of neurofibrillary tangles. It is as if the brain's wires got crossed and re-crossed, ultimately making it hard for these individuals to communicate verbally. Forming new memories becomes difficult. The person's behavior becomes out of sync and in conflict with those around them. Their wandering thoughts are accompanied by wandering bodies, and trouble integrating into our modern society begins.

There are many interesting phenomena surrounding this disease. I am not sure that all individuals who carry the diagnosis have the same entity that Alois Alzheimer described. Those first patients were relatively young. Science, with its attempts to medicalize all issues, has once again extended what was initially a fairly defined, probably in part genetically determined disease. Now according to some "scientific" criteria, up to 50% of people 85 years of age could carry this label. Considering our aging population, that is a lot of people.

How would you feel if you were 85 and you read you had a one-in-two chance of having this problem? Pretty scary, huh?

The next mysterious observation involves a paradox. Many patients found to have the nerve tangles do not have a significant life-interfering problem with memory. The findings in the brain suggest that they should have a problem but they do not.

The next observation should be humbling to any physician treating this disease with the current crop of Alzheimer's medications.

If you start medications like Aricept, Exelon, or Namenda early and measure certain activities of daily living, another paradoxical observation is noted. Even though they can dress themselves easier, go to the bathroom with less assistance, feed themselves with less difficulty, ultimately, there is no difference in when the patient is put into a nursing home or assisted living facility. Functionally, from society's standpoint, these medications have helped very little and are very expensive.

In my own nursing home practice, families of my patients were extremely reluctant when I suggested stopping these medications. Understandably, they felt frustrated that at the point their mother entered the nursing home, there was little that could be done with medications to help the situation. In fact, the opposite is true. One of the features of this phenomenon is the frequent increase in disorientation once mother is taken out of her little world and put into another quite unfamiliar one. Much like a child of two or three, she becomes frightened. Frequently, she will hoot and holler just like Mamma Mia crying out for her mother.

The disease already interferes with reasoning, so physicians resort to the use of sedatives to calm them down, Sometimes in high enough doses, they succeed. Surprise, surprise, the use of these drugs to sedate somebody like Mamma Mia just aggravates the problem of loss of mobility and communications skills. They have more difficulty in swallowing, so they choke more and, with a decrease in fluids, dehydration is more likely. Guess what happens? The patient is more likely to die sooner if we treat an absolutely normal behavioral response with powerful drugs initially developed to treat an entirely different problem, that of psychosis.

We are treating these people with the real and normal biological emotion of fear as if they were crazy. Something is very wrong with this picture.

Beginning in 1972 with Mamma Mia until February of 2007, I have taken care of a large number of patients whom I labeled with the diagnosis of dementia of the Alzheimer's type. I did not have brain tissue to go by, so I punted like most physicians dealing with this problem and stuck them in a "box".

I repeat here that scientists and physicians like to put people in a diagnostic "box" because it makes us feel better about our understanding of the world. Then like shopaholic Becky, whom I referred to earlier, ***not***.

I have a dear surgeon friend whom I was visiting with one day not long before I retired from hospital practice. We were discussing a patient I had with the Alzheimer's label. Larry said, "Joe, I'm not so sure it's a disease as much as it a phenomenon." After dealing with it for thirty-seven years, I agree. Like Scott Peck, M.D., I think Alzheimer's as well as most other chronic illnesses are psycho-social, economic, genetic, spiritual problems. They are not just one thing. Rarely does a disease fit squarely into the box we try to place it in.

Alzheimer's and the Industrial Age

Why is this phenomenon occurring so much more frequently? What is going on here?

To go back to the origins of this "disease," we will need to look farther back than you might expect. This actually applies to all dementing diseases. Below is a summary of most of the factors that have brought this phenomenon to our doorsteps.

When we were an agrarian society in America, Alzheimer's was not a big problem. First, life expectancy was age 50 as recently as 1900. The farmer and his wife did not live long enough to find out if their grade school education and parents had sentenced them to this mind-robbing problem. Purpose was not high on their priority list; they were just trying to grow enough food to feed themselves and that passel of kids they had. No contraception meant big families. Eight to ten kids making it to adulthood was not that uncommon out there in the rolling hills of Iowa.

As mechanization of farming in the mid-1800s increased crop yields, you had more kids than you needed to tend the farm. They needed jobs and those jobs were in the cities where they were building all that farm equipment and making all the fertilizers to increase the soil's yields. So the kids went off to the city, leaving mom and dad at home. Maybe not all the kids left, but more and more did. Some stayed to help gather the eggs, milk the cows, and farm the land with the folks. Most were not formally educated past the first few years of school, where they learned to read and write, mostly making sure they could sign their name and read the family Bible.

At that time, the social center of activity in the small towns close to the farms was the church. You had your weddings, funerals, christenings, and baptizing. Social life with no radio, television, or computers revolved around church functions as they danced and shared from the bounty of their harvest and had a good ole mutton supper now and then.

At night when the chores were completed, mom would reverently pull out that worn old family Bible and place it in the hands of a child who could read. When the problems and heartaches of life came, solace and understanding came from the scripture. Even if it were not read frequently or "deeply," it was still the main source of comfort and instruction. Existential doubt was not a big problem in Ozula, Iowa, at that time. If Mom or Dad "got down" with something, there was not much you could do but pray.

Working on the farm had another benefit. You got comfortable with death. It was just a part of everyday life. You got to see plenty of birth, from the seed you sowed to the baby chickens, pigs and occasional calf. But you got to see death up close and personal. And when that time came and it involved a loved one, you leaned on what you learned in the Bible to help you get through it.

Life on the farm was busy, sun-up to sun-down. Insomnia was not too big of a problem even when you had six to eight people sleeping in small quarters. Your bunkmates were physically tired, too.

Now the kids who moved to the city did not find a bed of roses, certainly not at the start of the twentieth century. There was not a social safety net and it was pretty much a dog-eat-dog world with the more educated rising to the top of the food chain. But city life had its allure. There were more things to do, places to go. And though you worked ten hours a day, it was not twelve and there were all those lights.

Lights everywhere. Shoot, you could go out after work instead of going home, eating a bite of supper and dropping into bed. There was drinking and dancing and smoking, bars and sporting events. That was your social life. The center of social activity was the boarding house. It became your family. Churches were to be found in the city but they were no longer the center of your social life, at least not like they were back on the farm.

Not constrained by distances, scant population densities and the watchful eyes of their mothers and fathers, kids did what most kids in their early reproductive biology-driven years do. They would try one shoe and if it didn't fit, they would just try another. Life in the city was exciting and busy. Night life added to the excitement but also to the problems, and when they came, the minister was a little harder to find. But you could now find help in magazines, books and newspapers, all vying for your attention. The family unit scattered and the security of home and church slowed eroded.

Time passed and agriculture became even more efficient. More kids moved away to work in the automobile factories and, during the two World Wars, in the plane and bomb factories. It was all happening so fast, not just in the United States, but all around the world. As more mouths needed to be fed, new strains of seeds were developed. But the problem was that over time and with the loss of the old hybrid vigor, the plants grew susceptible to pests. The pests had to go, so insecticides were developed by some of those kids who had left the farm. Problem was, nobody had time to study the effects of those organophosphates on the brains of the people living in and around Ozula, Iowa. Scientists said, "Trust us, we know what we're doing." Farms became less numerous, but larger, and cities grew in population.

Now when Mom and Dad "got down," there was not anybody left to take care of them. By now, the kids in the cities had families of their own. The grandchildren needed an education in order to rise to the top of the food chain. It took both husband and wife working to make ends meet. Cable TV, the Internet service, two car payments, mortgage on the house and credit card bills added to the demand for money, while soccer practice, dancing lessons and band added to the demand for time.

Who had time to deal with broken-down Mom and Dad back on the farm? Eventually Dad dies, leaving Mom alone on the farm. Now the kids get worried that something might happen to the now aged Mom out there by herself. And though Mom is not afraid of dying, the kids are. You see, as they have become part of the city, they are not used to having death and dying as a normal part of everyday experience. Oh, they may see plenty of it on TV or the movies, but it's usually violent and unnatural, so they don't feel comfortable with it like old Mom down on the farm. Interestingly, Mom does not really seem to be afraid of anything and that puzzles the kids. They just cannot understand it.

Projecting into the future some terrible scene of Mom falling, hurting herself and dying and them being so far away, one of the kids brings Mom into the city to live with her. Now when Mom gets to the city, she is fit as a fiddle. She still misses old Dad but with the help of the Bible and her church family, her grief is passing. The problem is she now has nothing to do. The house is nice enough but her children will not let her do anything and it just does not feel like home. The noise from the TV starts to make her nervous and she begins to get a little sad. She misses her church and her sewing club friends. She misses the chickens and her dogs. The dogs were too big and, besides, the grandchildren are allergic.

Mom starts to forget things, not the long ago things but the more recent things, especially since she moved to the daughter's house. The daughter gets worried and suspects Mom may be getting Alzheimer's. She read about it a few months ago in the *Ladies Home Journal* and then again in *Prevention* magazine. The next stop is the doctor's office.

The doctor asks her some questions and has a nurse give her a test drawing clocks and subtracting numbers. Nobody asks Mom what she can remember or about her church life or how she feels about coming to the city. X-rays of the brain are ordered and Mom is started on an antidepressant and a new pill for her memory. Quite a coincidence, the antidepressant is the same one the daughter is taking. The daughter started her medication when Mom moved in. Dealing with her mom had made her irritable and she felt guilty about those feelings. But, heck, she had a job, husband and two children to worry about. She was also a little more than miffed at her siblings for not stepping up to the plate to help with old Mom.

Mom did not improve much after seeing the doctor. She just seemed to gradually pull into her own little world. Some days she would just sit and say, "If I just had something to do!!" She felt so useless, she had no purpose. She began to pray for God to take her. She didn't say anything to her daughter; she knew it would just upset her.

She ate less and less, staying in bed more and more. Then bed-wetting began. Her daughter, having no experience in the process of dying, just got irritated. She had trouble seeing her mom as a two-year-old but felt guilty about her angry thoughts. She didn't tell anybody about the feelings of wishing her mother would die; the guilt and shame were too much.

Somewhat reluctantly, but feeling overwhelmed, she decided she would place her mother in a nursing home where, she convinced herself, her mother would get "better care." Within a few months, old Mom was barely recognizable. She had stopped eating and they were giving her Ensure and pureed food with a syringe. She also had a Foley catheter. Infections started in the lungs and bladder and the back-and-forth trips to the hospital began.

One day two years after Mom went into the nursing home, she died. Nobody was around except the nursing home staff, which was almost immune to the pathos of the scene. They had never known Mom back on the farm, vigorous, God-fearing and happy even after old Dad died.

Cause of death listed: Alzheimer's.

Real cause of death: Kids moving to the city from Ozula, Iowa.

Mom's perspective on cause of death: Body no longer had a purpose in communication. It had nothing left to say or do.

Manner of death: Inability of city kids to understand and deal with the experience of an inevitable process.

The saddest thing about this story is how it trivializes Mom's life. The children did not get to see all the loving acts that Mom performed on the farm. All the baked pies and meals for the farm next door when they were experiencing hard times. All the visits Mom made to her friends when they were sick in the 12-bed Ozula hospital. All of the little acts of kindness that Mom had done for the stranger whose car broke down a mile from the farm.

Obviously, I do not think Mom had a good death. I would not want it for myself or for you, but this story is being repeated thousands of times every day in America. It is a tremendous burden on an already-overloaded medical system. We have all played a role in bringing this phenomenon about. Who in this picture needs forgiveness? We all do.

Nursing Home Prevention Plan

I believe we can rewrite this picture. I do not believe it has to be this way. The answer comes from above and I do not mean the federal government. I mean WAY above. There is no secular answer to the problem of dementia. I will even go out on a limb here and say that all the scientists, all the drug companies, all the government insurance programs and all the private medical insurance plans are not going to fix this problem. Not only are they not going to fix the problem, they cannot fix it. Why?

Because at its essence, the care of the elderly is a spiritual problem. It is a relationship problem. It is a fear of death problem.

And what is more, I think we all know somewhere deep within us the truth of who we really are. The truth not just in our own individual lives but those of our brothers and sisters. This truth of which I am speaking is not a biological sense but a Biblical sense. The truth is we are all special in God's eyes. And as we consider that truth, there is no better place to start in dealing with the care of the aged than with one of Christ's most repeated teachings: Do unto others as you would have them do to you. It is actually a statement of fact. It will be done to you as you have done to others. Let that sink in. Pretty sobering isn't it? You children out there listen. Your own children are watching you and you can teach them some of life's most beautiful lessons by how you handle your own parents' frailties.

Rules of Living to Prevent Dementia

Below are some ideas I have come to believe will help you or a loved one avoid the Alzheimer's phenomenon. Not completely, but it sure will tilt the odds in your favor.

#1. Keep moving. Your physical movement signals the neutral body that the mind is still active and has plans. Many studies show decreased risk of Alzheimer's disease in the long-time physically active. Activity actually causes new brain sprouts and connections.

#2. Have a purpose. The less the purpose has to do with you and your own little melodrama, the better. Placing the purpose in the context of serving others ensures you will always have something to do. Pray for a servant's heart.

#3. Stay connected. It is a well-known fact that people who are more socially involved have less of a problem with this phenomenon. When I say connected, I don't mean climbing the social ladder. That is not connection, that is competition. Competition is your natural biological state and that does not help with this problem. I mean, see everybody you meet or see as a potential person to help.

#4. Let others help you. Prideful independence quite frequently and perversely hastens physical dependence at the end of life. Some of the most beautiful absolute saints in my life have been found in nursing homes. Their neutral body may be worn out but their minds are not. It is not nursing homes that are the problem. It is what they are used for that is.

#5. Do not use the body for pleasure. Smoking and excess alcohol are major risk factors for dementia. So are some of the more common tranquilizers. They interfere with the processing of information, both old and new.

#6. Learn to live in the present moment. It is the only place you will find lasting happiness. Stress and worry increase some of the hormones that make your brain not work as well. Depression is a major risk factor for dementia among other problems.

#7. Learn to laugh. Particularly at yourself. Serious people tend to believe falsely that they are in control. I hope you recognize by now, that is a big lie. God is. His will for you is true happiness.

#8. Stop worrying about what you eat. This was the hardest rule for me to swallow. I had spent nearly thirty years of my medical career harping at people about what they should not eat. That was nonsense. It took a real "Come to Jesus Meeting" to get me to see things differently. Overeating is the problem. You are using the body for pleasure. It was not intended for that. Obesity and diabetes frequently are due to overeating and they are both risk factors for dementia.

#9. Remember we are in this together. Literally. If you end up with dementia, do not worry about it. John Newton, the famous minister who penned "Amazing Grace," developed a memory problem in his later years. It might have been due to his excesses of his youth or genes, I do not know. When his parishioners called his attention to the wandering nature of his sermons, he replied, "I remember two things. I am a great sinner, but He's a great Savior."

In the end, if you find that your memory is not that of your youth, try keeping John Newton's facts in mind. It will make the passing more pleasant.

Chapter 12

There Are No Geniuses at the Top to Fix Our Problem

Thank you Lord for hiding these things from the wise and prudent and revealing them to babes.
Jesus in Matthew 11:25

But what certainty is there about money, which after all, holds all the world together? It depends on the good will of a few capitalists to keep to the agreement that one metal is worth more than another.
Ivan Krueger, Swiss industrialist
who committed suicide in 1932

It is as dangerous to be sentenced by a Physician as by a judge.
Sir Thomas Browne,
English physician and writer (1605-1682)

If life is an illusion, then so is death - the greatest illusion of all. If life must not be taken too seriously, then neither must death.
Samuel Butler, 1835-1901, English Writer

Happy the people whose annals are blank in history books.
Thomas Carlyle, 1795- 1881, Scottish historian and sociologic writer

195

I have come close to the end of my confessions. I have just a few more. This chapter will confirm I have not totally given up on the idea of being the fixer. You know there is one in every crowd.

My wife would be only too happy to tell you I have an opinion on everything. I mean everything. This book is a classic example.

In the setting of a patient-doctor encounter, particularly primary care, the physician is constantly being asked, "Well, doc, what should I do?" I became the specialist in "Dr. Joe's opinion," which really could be an alternate title for these encounters. For that matter, the title of this book.

It is a hard role to give up, especially if you like people and want to help them. The vast majority of physicians would never choose primary care medicine if they did not like people. You can trust that, at the heart level, your personal physician likes you, even loves you. I am talking that philos (friendship) type of love that says that even in the midst of this overwhelming problem we are facing in health care today, he or she has your physical best interests in mind when they try to answer the question, "What should I do?" When mistakes are made, and there are many, the doctor does not consciously intend you harm. It was most frequently an error in judgment. I make them, you make them, your doctor makes them. Remember, not just in medicine, we are in this thing we call life together.

We are also in this health care crisis together. It is not occurring in a vacuum. It is a part of a much bigger crisis, a psycho - economic - socio - educational - spiritual crisis. Due to the widespread use of technology in communication, we are getting a bird's-eye view that all is not well with the world. To believe the power of positive thinking or a secular humanist approach is going to get us out of this pickle and solve the world's problems and health care crisis is simply denial. That is not just "Doctor Joe's opinion." It is an opinion I share with my Guide. Nor is it a hastily drawn opinion. I have been mulling this one over for at least the last twenty years and I believe that if Homo sapiens as a species with all its vast powers of communication and technology are to survive on this blue planet called Earth, it will take a miracle.

I am not talking about the kind of miracle that I often refer to when using my cell phone. Although I admit when I am talking to my mother in the Rio Grande Valley while I am hiking the mountains of Colorado, I am impressed. I do stand in awe of the incredible power that comes from man's mind to accomplish some phenomenal feats. Certainly, the instructional sciences of math, physics and engineering have wrought many wonders and the power of community to bring them into being is amazing.

To digress a moment, at one time I, too, worshiped the god of science and I understand how it can cloud the vision of many of our brother and sister "experts" today. However, looking back on my life, I fortunately never experienced "reverential awe" when using any of the burden-lifting tools and toys of science of technology. I have been blessed with a healthy skepticism of the offerings of modern science all of my professional career.

The required miracle to survive I refer to is of the supernatural variety. It is the type of miracle recorded in the lives of saints and an extension of the miracle evident in the historic story of Therese Neuman. God will again have to invade the time-space continuum that makes up the history of the species we call Homo sapiens in order to save this means of communicating His love. Simply put, He will have to step in to save us from our own self-destruction. Otherwise, the smart guys had better start training crickets and cockroaches in how to use cell phones, PCs and all this other technology for when man, the Homo sapiens man, is gone.

If you want to see what the descriptive sciences of biology and anthropology have to say in more detail about the fate of the species, read the works of Robert Sapolsky and Melvin Konner.

These guys are not just good scientists, they are brilliant scientists. Robert Sapolsky's *The Primate's Memoir*, and *Why Zebras Don't Get Ulcers* should be required reading for all first-year medical and divinity students.

The Tangled Wing by Melvin Konner deserves its place of honor, as it is a breathtaking panoramic view and description of human behavior.

These two guys are geniuses at seeing, in fact, just how this perceptual world is. One slight problem: Their secular solutions to the problems they see will not work. Secretly, between you and me, I do not really believe they believe their secular answers for the survival of the species. Oh, maybe short-term, but long-term, no way. The crickets and cockroaches are going to have to learn to read their books as well as this simple one. It will not be man without supernatural help.

Medicine has its own set of experts and technological geniuses. I know. I was trained by some of the best. Some of the things that have come out of the medical sciences are show-stoppers. Laparoscopic and robotic surgery are just two examples of the amazing ingenuity of the human brain. The artificial heart is pretty darned impressive. Joint replacements are an incredible gift of some of the best minds in the world.

X-ray imaging devices, CT, MRI, PET scans, have proven to be technological wonders saving many lives as they explore the body and its workings. If properly used, they can save bodies and unnecessary surgeries. Improperly used, they are a misery both personally and to somebody's pocketbook.

Medical technology has outstripped our ability to pay for it as a nation. At the current rate of demand, we cannot pay for all the wants of all the people who view health care as a right without going further and further into debt as a nation. The numbers simply do not compute. The current demand is unsustainable.

The financial geniuses at the top are right about that, and there are some financial geniuses at the top levels of government. Heck, even the political geniuses know that it is unsustainable. Yes, we are just full of geniuses, financial, scientific and political. Those same political geniuses are members of Congress and they understand the huge sums required to pay for the medical wants of an aging and frequently fearful populace.

There just ain't enough money. You can fire up those printing presses. Ben Bernanke can order all the G-10s at the Department of the Treasury to work as much overtime as he wants to. You still cannot meet the unrestricted demands of a death-fearing people. Ultimately, you will break the bank, not just America's bank, but that of other countries as well.

I am in complete agreement with President Obama that solving America's health care crisis is essential to solving not only America's economic problem, but it is essential to solving the upcoming global problems. Like it or not, we are all in this together. And when I say "we," I am not restricting myself to our national boundaries.

The problem in medical care today is like someone who has advanced cancer. The patient, our current medical sick care system, is terminally ill. I occasionally have had to tell the patient, "You are sick, really sick. You're not too sick to operate on, but you are too sick NOT to operate on." That is where we are today. We need major surgery on this current system.

Now I am a pretty detached unbiased guy when it comes to the medical care crisis or, at least, I have not hidden my biases. My economic bias is that I think the current mechanism of exchange with its use of paper and plastic (debit not credit card) to pay for services or goods beats the old barter system. I also think the current use of paper and plastic is more civilized than the use of precious metals. I certainly think that going back to the exchange of precious metals would just hasten the stripping away of the thin veneer of civilization. Our current financial system just makes life easier and more convenient. But I really do not think it is overstating the case to say that if we do not take some radical steps in solving this dilemma now, you and I could be using chickens, eggs and heaven knows what else as a means of monetary exchange a lot sooner than anybody currently thinks.

If history is any guide, this bleak picture is an inevitable outcome of fiat currencies. They might be able to tolerate that over in Zimbabwe, but I am not sure that my rather soft friends here in the USA would be able to cope as well. I do not think our genius economists are going to be of much help if things go that far. I know the geniuses at the top know what I am saying is a fairly accurate picture of what just might happen if we do not fix the problem. They do not want to tell you because they do not want to start a stampede. Unfortunately, they do not know how to fix it.

Is the cavalry coming and who are they?

You are the cavalry. We are the cavalry and we can fix this problem. This is a bottom-up fixing, not a top-down fixing.

Where do we start?

Demand for medical services can be traced back to the idea that you do not have any control over your illnesses. PLEASE!!!!!! If you have read this far, I know that you know, deep-down inside you, and maybe not so deep down, this fact. In many cases, in perhaps over half the cases, **_you_** are responsible for the illnesses you have. I am not talking about your kids with their infectious diseases, childhood cancers, and rare genetic defects. I am talking about the bulk of chronic diseases in adults swamping our medical system and putting it into the medical bind it is in. I am saying they are largely self-induced and, in fact, trace their origins to our own selfishness. I am telling you this because I love you and call you friend, and sometimes friends have to tell friends things they do not want to hear.

Most "illnesses" you have are because you are lazy and want your own way. That is the unvarnished truth. I am not running for president of the United States and I am not trying to build a medical practice. I like my quiet life, but I do want to tell you as my friend. You can get mad at me, you can call me crazy. It's okay. But I am telling you that most of your illnesses come from your desire to be right, to have what seems to be your own way. And you are too mentally and then physically lazy (notice the order) to do anything about it. At least, not consistently.

It is simply too easy to blame the world, the politicians, your husband, your wife, your father, mother, kids, race, gender or genetics or just bad luck for your illnesses. A pill is easier to swallow than the idea you are sick because you want to be sick.

I hope I have made it clear that none of us knows what we are doing. Our behavior is for the large part driven by very primitive parts of our brain. It is a fact that you are actually aware of your behavior after it is done or in progress. In a sense, our lives are giant rationalizations.

Rationalization is the retrospective assigning to our behavior reasons for the behavior, and most often, we choose to put a good spin on it so as to present the face of innocence. Ultimately, whether you are able to admit it or not, you choose your illnesses and, in most cases, the mode of exit for the body. You choose how you are going to die. Let me repeat here that I said at least fifty percent of all illnesses, but not all. But without each of us admitting that we play a large role in many of the illnesses we ask the medical system to fix, there will be no end to the health care crisis. Decreasing demand is the only fiscally sustainable way out, and you have a huge say.

You changing your thinking is the only hope of a cavalry to deliver you. The change in your thinking is not easy but is possible. I like to think of it as the narrow road Jesus spoke of in Matthew when He said, "Enter by the narrow gate; for the gate is wide and the way is broad that leads to destruction, and many are those who enter by it. For the gate is small, and the way is narrow that leads to life, and few are those who find it." Fortunately, you have help traveling down this road in the form of the Holy Spirit or Guide we have talked about.

From a practical standpoint, I am asking you, even begging you, to consider the following: On your way to your next doctor's appointment or on your way to the emergency room for a nonemergent condition, ask yourself these questions: Am I angry at somebody? Am I holding on to resentment against my brother? Is there anybody that I can call to mind that I haven't forgiven? Here's the payoff. By looking on your brothers and sisters with forgiveness, you will start the process of solving the health care crisis. The miracle in your own improving health will begin immediately. You will treat the problem where the problem is. The problem is usually in your mind and that is where the healing needs to start.

One Sunday a few years ago, Bob Murphy, a local East Texas humorist, called across the church parking lot, "Hey doc, you got any good medical advice for me?" "Yeah, Bob, don't get sick!" The best way for you to do your part in the health care crisis is to not get sick in the first place. Cultivating a forgiving heart is the best place to start.

Doctors Need Forgiveness, Too

The scene was late winter or early spring of 1972 and I was surrounded by the medical staff of Mass General Hospital. As a prospective intern, I had to pass an interview conducted by a group of academic physicians. There were several distinguished looking doctors in attendance.

I was nervous as evidenced by my sweating palms and slightly elevated heart rate. They did their best to put me at ease asking about my personal life, wife, children, where I grew up. No specific questions to check my fountain of knowledge, just casual questions about this and that. Then the bomb: "Mr. Davis, what do you think is the biggest problem facing medicine today?" "What?" I wanted to shout but didn't. If they had asked me the seven most common metabolic causes of coma, I would not have blinked an eye. My brain was crammed full of facts all the way to the brim. But noooooo, they asked me to think, and for the prior four years, I had done little of that. I had been too busy learning just the facts.

I remember as though it were yesterday the absolute feeling of being caught with my pants down. I do not remember if I blushed or turned pale, but in an instant, I thought my hopes of coming to this institution are over, so I blurted something out. That something was this: "I think the biggest problem facing medicine today is the ability of the physician to maintain intellectual honesty in the face of increasing government control." Now I do not know if they recorded that conversation in 1972, but leaving out the "ers" and "uhs," that is exactly what I said. You know, when people ask you about your most embarrassing moment, the answer I gave and still give today is that story. I remember walking out of that interview kicking myself for blowing it, for being such a pompous ass. But those gentlemen conducting the interview must have been quite tolerant, as they did allow me to come there to do my postgraduate training.

I learned more than one lesson that day, as I have recalled the painful event many times since. First, be prepared to think. Stop, listen, hear, then speak. These are the steps in true thinking.

The second lesson I learned was that it is perfectly okay to say, "I don't know." In fact, it is probably the truest thing that any of us can say. We don't KNOW. We can have an opinion but we really do not know.

In retrospect, I am pretty sure that was also my most humbling moment. Despite the fact I had no clue as to what I was saying that day, it has turned out to be very close to being correct.

The Golden Rule and the Doctor/Patient Relationship

As I said earlier, you can trust that your primary care doctor not only likes you, but, I suspect, loves you. I am speaking generally; I know there may be rare exceptions.

C. S. Lewis points out in *Mere Christianity,* that there is a principle that operates between two people when they come together. It is a sense of fair play and probably comes from the intuitive recognition that the other fellow is not all that different from you. Even in those who would call themselves nonbelievers, it still seems to operate somehow. Somewhere deep within us, we know the truth of the "golden rule" and that is why you will find some variant of it in all the major religions.

It is my belief that it is not a brain thing, but a heart thing. Remember when I said your mind is not confined to your brain, but is also to be found in your heart? I am not speaking metaphorically here; I mean the pulsating organ in the center of your chest is part of your mind. I believe it to be the source of your intuition and where the truth of the "golden rule" resides and thus, the sense of fair play. I believe all encounters are holy if your "vision" is correct. With this in mind, let us consider the doctor/patient relationship.

For millennia, this relationship in all cultures has been considered sacred. On one side, you had the shamans, priests, and physicians. On the other side were the suffering, the ill, the patient. The healers were supposed to have special knowledge, other worldly knowledge, and a lot of superstition was involved. Unfortunately, there still is. Perhaps superstition is one of those words we had better define.

Superstition - *any belief or attitude based on fear or ignorance, that is inconsistent with the known laws of science or what is generally considered in the particular society as true and rational; esp. such a belief in charms, omens and the supernatural.*

Webster's Dictionary

Now listen carefully: I am telling you the current practice of medicine in the United States is rife with the above elements, those of superstition, but for many the word is used as an epithet.

What I am saying is that when you go to your doctor, you do so out of fear and ignorance. You go because you are sick and believe the doctor has special knowledge and "amulets" to get you better. Most of the time, the doctor realizes that, based on the laws of the known science, in general, your presenting physical complaint does not require anything to make you better.

Let us use a common example of upper respiratory infections. You go to the doctor with a cold. You're busy, you don't have time to be sick and you want to get better now. (Yesterday would have been better.) Most colds are caused by viruses and are not responsive to antibiotics, but the doctor, not always, but frequently, gives you a prescription for antibiotics and or an injection, pats you on the shoulder and sends you on your way. Down deep, he knows what he has just done is not according to the laws of medical science, but what the heck. It's not a big deal and you enjoy your magical thinking or magic of that antibiotic and/or shot. That, my friends, is superstition and it happens millions of times a day in offices across the country.

Let me give you another example. A 67-year-old retired dentist comes into my office. He wants his blood drawn. His brother had surgery recently for prostate cancer and he wants to check his PSA. This blood test is often used quite inappropriately to "diagnose" a very common cancer in men. "Science" has shown that there may actually be more problems with using the test than not. The "experts" do not agree. The reality is that there are a lot of scientific opinions. Since my father died at age 69 from prostate cancer and my brother had his prostate removed at the age of fifty-seven for the same, it is fair to say I have more than just a casual interest in this issue.

I explained all this to my dentist friend and suggested he subject himself to a digital rectal exam if he were truly interested in an accurate screening, knowing full well there is a host of other screening tests available, including prostate ultrasound and free PSA levels, etc. Although it had been five years since his last digital rectal exam and this was his first time to see me, he felt uncomfortable and refused. The dentist came to my office in fear and ignorance, afraid that he might have the same disease as his brother.

Even though I consider myself well read on the topic, I have to confess I do not really **know** what the best course is for screening and treating this most common cancer of older men. The dentist is fearful and ignorant; I am just ignorant. By the definition I have used above, any advice I could give my dentist friend on what he should do is based on superstition, not truth.

But I do believe there is a truth that is not relative here, that is not based on any current scientific opinions. That truth is the presence of the golden rule that operates between the dentist and me. I genuinely want what is best for his life because what is best for his life is best for mine. They are not separate. That, in fact, is what the golden rule teaches: We are one. That would be considered supernatural to the world's eyes and to the scientific experts' eyes and, therefore, any advice I might give to my dentist friend would be seen as superstitious. And according to the definition above, I would agree. The Golden Rule is operating in this office encounter.

Government Control and the Golden Rule

Medicine is in grave danger of losing its heart where the Golden Rule #1 is etched. I have quickly sketched a couple of examples to give you just a hint of the potential problems that exist today and which portend of even bigger problems tomorrow.

Remember, the 1st Golden Rule: " Do unto others as you would have them do unto you." The 2nd Golden Rule is: "He who pays the gold makes the rules." You and I both know this from personal experience. We all work for somebody, even those of us who are self-employed. Your boss pays you wages, and if he or she is not satisfied with your performance, you get fired. Although some rules may be implied and not written down, there is a mutual understanding between you and your employer regarding performance for pay. You may not always agree but for the most part, we consider this agreement fair.

For millennia, the doctor/patient relationship has been sacred but has also involved the exchange of some type of payment for services rendered. These have included chickens, goats, eggs, wine, shells, stones and precious metals. For the last two hundred years, we have progressed rapidly from coin to paper to plastic to electronic photons.

Golden Rule # 3 enters the picture: "The love of gold (money) is the root of all kinds of evil." Although the rich may squirm a bit at this empirical observation, I think most would agree with this. Money can and does change your thinking. The presence of a lot of money can really change your thinking. This is the truth, and in our heart of hearts, we know it. It changes our brain thinking and, it is amazing what it does for our powers of rationalization. The truth is the higher you are on the food chain, the more money you seem to want. Not always, but nearly always.

Let me confess up front, I have been guilty of the sin of greed. I have had to work very hard to keep this desire in check. Let's face it: In our society, physicians are near the top of the food chain, and seldom do they have to worry about where their next meal is coming from.

This has not always been so. For most centuries, including a fair part of the twentieth century, physicians made a decent living, but not extravagant. As recently as the Great Depression, many physicians just got by. Nobody had any money and more times than not, the physician was given some baked goods or settled for a handshake or a hug. It was the golden age of primary care medicine, the years of the 1930s, '40s and even early '50s. The doctor of that day seemed kind and helpful. He knew his patients as friends. When they came to see him and it was time to present the bill, Doc knew Bob worked for a dollar an hour, had three kids and a pregnant wife, and, using the trustworthy Golden Rule #1, he charged accordingly. And that wonderful sense of fair play worked both ways. If Doc made a mistake, as he occasionally did, Bob did not sue him. They worked things out. And is it not amazing how eye-to-eye contact with your patients can keep the ol' greed bug in check; it works like a charm. It is one of those things that cannot be measured, but sure counts.

That all started to change right after World War II. We were the most powerful industrialized society on earth. All those returning servicemen got jobs and, to keep wages down at the re-cranked-up auto factories, Congress set up laws allowing for the exclusion of health insurance benefits for the auto workers and a new industry took off, private health insurance. It might not have been the first nail in the coffin, but we saw the lid closing on the coffin of our idea of Marcus Welby, M.D. Like a Trojan horse, we allowed private insurance into the examination room and thus began the slow destruction of one of man's most vital and beautiful trusts, the operation of the Golden Rule #1. It depends on face-to-face interaction.

Private insurance grew and the government's Medicare insurance plan, started in 1965, was not far behind. Slowly, the practice of medicine changed as the responsible party paying for the physician's services changed. Instead of Doc and Bob working something out eye-to-eye, a faceless corporate or government entity slowly eased its way between the two.

Medicine became less of an art and more and more a cold calculating capitalist enterprise. Golden Rule #2 insinuated itself into this relationship and the rule book began to thicken. Paperwork and then computer work began to dominate. The doctor had less and less time to spend visiting with his friend as the administrative burdens of the practice grew. New technology flourished, some quite sensational and even helpful, but the majority added little to the overall clinical outcome. Over all, sick people did not become healthier. It just became more expensive to get sick, and making unbiased decisions in the medical office became increasingly difficult.

Golden Rule #3 is now playing itself out to the unsurprising nightmare in which we find ourselves today. Like it or not, primary care physicians have become businessmen detaching themselves from the "heart" of the profession they claim, and they are not very happy. In a recent survey, over half of all currently active primary care physicians do not plan to be in practice within three years.

I quit my traditional medical insurance-based practice over two years ago. For me the practice of medicine had simply become too crazy. If you could enter into the back office of your primary care physician today, you would be amazed at the sensory overload to which he or she is exposed. They are literally being bombarded from every possible direction. The gate keeper's job is overwhelming. You have heard the saying, "Manure flows downhill." It does, right smack-dab into the middle of the primary care physician's office.

Remember when I said that selfishness is the father of all sin? You would scarcely believe the amount of selfishness that works through your primary care doc's office. "What about me?" is the reigning cry.

Patients request expensive exams they do not need and medications they have read about in some popular magazine or seen on television. Pharmacy managers from as far away as Canada are faxing or calling for changes in drugs as their formularies change. Medical durable supply companies are requesting a qualifying diagnosis so they can drink deeply from the breast of Medicare. Home health care agencies are wanting an OK for extension of services beyond that which the doctor thinks is appropriate. Nursing homes call to report that Mamma Mia has fallen out of bed for the umteenth time, just to let you know. They are required by the state to inform you. Hospitals are calling with "no doc" call admissions as more and more people migrate to the ER for their primary care as the number of physicians willing to put up with this madness dwindles.

210

In all this, to expect the physician to act in the patient's best interest without succumbing to Golden Rule #3 (the love of money) is idiocy. Jesus said, "Why are you worried about the speck in your brother's eye when you have a board in your own?" Responsibility and compassion must work both ways.

Forgiveness Applies to All

I have been saying throughout this book, you need to forgive first, and then you will be granted understanding. Here, I am asking your forgiveness for myself and my physician colleagues for having trouble maintaining intellectual honesty in the face of increasing government and insurance company control.

For myself, I do have trouble keeping my composure when I hear the prescription for this madness from the "geniuses" at the top. And I have to say to all of you so-called "experts" committed to a universal health insurance plan, you do not have a clue as to what is really going on here. In fact, you are the blind trying to lead the blind.

One of the most pernicious beliefs is that electronic medical records will somehow fix this problem. Sitting in an exam room with a computer terminal and trying to type while trying to truly listen to what the patient is saying is asking the impossible of the physician. Listening is at the heart of the healing process. It takes face-to-face, eye-to-eye, undivided attention and it is an ***art*** acquired over many years of practice. Electronic medical records are one step further in the wrong direction. It is one more step in worshiping the god of the intellect and one more step toward cutting the heart out of medicine.

To those experts who think more "science" is going to make us healthier, I say you are ignorant. Science may be able to help us with our symptoms, but it will not and cannot fix our problems. Your judgment is so clouded by Golden Rule #2 (he who has the gold makes the rules), you can no longer see. You have lost any semblance of intellectual honesty. You who jump into the wagon in hopes of getting your share of the pie to maintain your position at the top of the food chain have ensured that. Financial self-interest keeps you fettered to the drug companies, biotech companies and insurance companies as it stomps down any moral compromise you might feel. The unstated goal to medicalize human behavior and come up with a pill to treat it is the exact opposite of the "love thy neighbor as thyself" commandment. By your work you make people more fearful and encourage their false beliefs in a solution outside their own heart. You project onto them your own fear of death. Golden Rule #1 says you will pay a price for this and it should give you pause. Jesus said, "Whatever you do to the least of these, you do to me." I believe He meant what He said.

What Should I Do, Doctor Joe?

As I have indicated throughout this book, in my opinion, these three questions are worthy of your consideration. I believe your ultimate happiness and the abundant life the Lord wants you to have depends upon your asking and finding the answer to them.

Who am I?
What am I doing here?
What am I supposed to do?

In my reading, people have been asking these questions for a long time. We were and are perplexed by these different natures

212

that seem to live within us. Sometimes the devil, sometimes the saint. I decided to conduct an imaginary interview with Jesus to see what He might give as His answers to these questions.

Questions and Answers - An Interview with Jesus

About two thousand years ago, God felt our brain and heart were ready for true answers, the Best answers He could give. He sent His Son Jesus, who invaded our time space continuum to answer our questions. I believe His answers to you and me today are the same answers He gave 2000 years ago.

Who are we?

"It depends on what you choose to do. If you choose to believe in me, you can follow me, identify with me and be mine. You no longer belong to yourself, you belong to me. You are now a host to God. And even though I know terrible things are happening on this Planet Earth, I will show you how to see things differently so that while you are walking around here, you can actually be happy. I mean everlastingly happy. Indeed, there will always be mischief and things you think you have to worry about, but I'm telling you, it's going to be okay. For you who believe in me, a happy outcome is certain in all things. This I promise; I give you my word. All the medical care crises in this world won't amount to a hill of beans in the long run. So chill. You are mine and we are one. I still see the rest of the folks as my brothers, though they may not recognize me yet."

Why are we here ?

"To wake up to the answer to Question #1. You may think you came here to Planet Earth to be a doctor, lawyer, minister, teacher, housewife, politician, or engineer. Sorry, you came here to be mine. You came to be my brother, my friend. Why? I need your help. I see the suffering and the weeping and the gnashing of the teeth that you see. Nothing much has changed since I was here last. Oh, the means of destruction of the body have become more 'sophisticated,' but the means aren't important. There are more people, a lot more people, and that could be a problem in the not-so-distant future, but as with the health care crisis, you don't need to worry about the big picture. Our Father is in control of that; you just follow me. I want you to look around you in your ordinary life and help your brother and neighbor. It was the best sociologic advice I could give 2000 years ago; I think it still works today."

What are we supposed to do?

" Remember when I said you came to wake up to our brotherhood. Even though it can happen quickly, it usually takes awhile, even years. I sent the Holy Spirit to help each of you as you adjust your thinking to this new world, this heaven on earth. He's a good Guide. Listen to Him. You can rely on Him to steer you in the right direction. But I'm going to tell you, it takes setting aside some quiet time for Him. He doesn't speak loudly; it doesn't seem to help Him get his point across. I'll tell you something else: You can't really spend too much time with Him. The more you listen, the better you become at hearing. He'll lead you to that irresistible future.

Let me straighten out a few other things before I have to go. Your brain is a pretty amazing piece of work, if I do say so myself. So is your heart. In fact, the whole body is pretty impressive, but it's not who you are. You know, it's not that you expect too much of yourself that bothers me; it's that you are satisfied with too little. I still think that comes from identifying with your body and its organs. Last point: You are Spirit and it's hard for me to help you understand that. Your Spirit has authority over the material world, not just the one you are living in, but all the stars and planets as well. I personally guarantee if you keep awakening, you will have some of these spiritual moments that will leave you awestruck, not unlike my visit with Paul on his road to Damascus. Most of you would be too frightened by that experience; so I have chosen the more gradual introduction instead. Remember, we are all in this together. Keep on forgiving, keep on loving one another, even the 'geniuses' at the top."

Well, that just about wraps it up. I say ditto to what Jesus says. One last thing: If on your road back to happiness and health you are tempted to take the apple back off the tree of knowledge of good and evil and go back to seeing the world through fearful biological eyes, remember this first line of an ancient anonymous hymn written in the 1300s in Ireland.

BE THOU MY VISION, OH LORD OF MY HEART

Let God be God and you be content to be His creation.

        Love,
          Dr. Joe

Epilogue

But the things that proceed out of the mouth come from the heart, and these defile the man. For out of the heart come evil thoughts, murders, adulteries, fornications, thefts, false witness, slanders.
Jesus, Matthew 15:18-19

For as he thinks within himself, so he is.
Proverbs 23:7a

"If you can think and not make thoughts your aim..." Rudyard Kipling and I agree about the two-edged sword that thinking represents. "Knowledge comes but wisdom lingers," is another truthful statement that gives us pause on reflection.

As I warned in the introduction, this is a book designed to make you think. It is my prayer that it has helped you to begin thinking correctly. Your thoughts do matter. There are no neutral thoughts. Your correct thinking ultimately leads to your sanity and on to happiness and peace of mind. These three are inseparable.

I also made the seemingly outlandish statement that your mind is not confined to your brain. You can, in fact, awaken to your ability to think with your heart. You have, unwittingly, been doing this all along. You have not always been aware of it.

The "scientific community" has often tried to explain away our Lord's words above, spoken in Matthew. One explanation cited is that since anatomy was not well known 2000 years ago, Jesus must have been referring to the subconscious mind still found in the gray and white matter locked in your and my skull. He could not possibly mean the mind was to be found anywhere else in your body.

Yet, Wilder Penfield, a world-famous neurobiologist and neurosurgeon, in his *Mystery of the Mind,* came to the conclusion that the workings of the brain cannot account for man's mind and thoughts.

I am telling you these things because I want you to have understanding and I want you to continue with your thinking - your own independent thinking. Too often, we allow others to do our thinking for us. I know I have. I believe this occurs because we, most often, are simply too lazy or slothful. It is easier to let somebody else do our thinking for us.

In my own case, especially early in my career, I bought into the idea that if a person had M.D., M.A., or Ph.D., after their name, they at least knew something about something. As I also pointed out, somewhere along the line, I realized none of us really knows anything with absolute certainty except as it relates to our own personal experiences - at least, when it comes to the knowledge derived from our five senses. We can certainly have opinions regarding the perceptual world we live in, but cannot have a communicable certain knowledge of the visible world because we did not create it.

Simply put, though there is a high degree of probability the sun will rise in the East tomorrow morning, I cannot say with 100% accuracy that it will not rise in the West. I cannot even say it will rise at all. One day the sun will burn out and no longer give its light. Oh, I realize the astrophysicists have assured us that this will probably take a few more billion years, but they cannot say with 100% certainty that it could not happen tomorrow. The physicists' predictions are based on this visible material world as being the limits of conceptual reality. Let me quickly add, there are a number of very bright scientists who realize the limitations of even the mathematically based instructional science of physics. The brightest of them are almost childlike in their contemplation of this mysterious and fabulously complex universe.

Kipling warns us not to make thoughts our aim and that is why I want to warn you not to stop with just thinking. I would encourage you to continue up the path of consciousness past your thinking, beyond symbols, beyond words, beyond sound. The paradox was given to us by our Master when He said that the Kingdom of Heaven does not come by observation, but comes from within you. As you progress in your spiritual journey to a "pure heart," that will become manifest as you cultivate a forgiving heart. You will "see" God.

I believe we need more healers and fewer physicians and I believe each of you has the capacity to be a healer. As I said before, all healing starts with the mind and the neutral body will generally follow quite nicely. I have suggested you learn something about your body, not because it is needed for your salvation, but because it is so terribly interesting.

If you have read this book, then I believe you are capable of reading and understanding a textbook of medical physiology. I have recommended Guyton's *Textbook of Medical Physiology*. It is commonly used at the college as well as the medical school level. I am sure there are others that would serve the purpose equally well.

The Teaching Company is another wonderful resource. They have a multitude of courses on various topics, including a course in human anatomy and physiology, complete with text, audio CD, and DVD aides. Their phone number is 1-800-832-2412. The Web site address is www.teach12.com.

Clearly, I believe the Bible is a must-read for anyone who wants to be "well". There are almost too many versions of this good book on the market. *The Story Bible* by Pearl S. Buck may be found at Amazon.com, in the used book category. As I indicated, it is a Cliff Notes version, but I think it is useful as an introduction. A popular modern-day language version is *The Message*.

Twenty years ago, a friend suggested that I should read the New Testament as a novel, straight through, without commentaries or study guides. I used a paperback copy I picked up at the airport for ten dollars and I think it was very useful. It convicted me of the historicity of what I had been told.

For several years I used the New Jerusalem Bible as my bedside companion. The language is more modern and, for some, may be a comfortable place to start.

At this point, I am not particular. In traveling, I will use the copy in the bedside table left by the Gideons. Parenthetically, I think the work done by the Gideons is tremendous. We definitely take the ready availability of the Bible for granted. There are many countries today, particularly those under previous Communist rule, where Bibles are scarce and pages are passed around like the valuable treasure that they are.

A Course in Miracles is a very profound book by Helen Schucman and William Thetford. I think it can be very useful to the right reader. "Right" in this context involves some judgment on my part. "Read at the right time" would probably be the more accurate term.

My first encounter with this title, *A Course in Miracles*, some twenty years ago, shortly after my divorce, came at a time when I was reading everything I could get my hands on to help me understand what was happening in my personal life. I picked up Gerald Jampolsky's *Good-bye to Guilt*. This is one of the many easier to read introductions to the Course but I did not pursue it further. Then, in 1990 at my 25th high school reunion, a good friend and an Episcopal priest, recommended that I read it. To do the

Course justice requires at least a year's commitment and I was unwilling to commit that much time to anything at that point. I was too busy trying to "cure" the world.

Fast forward to the spring of 2003. I had undergone the born-again conversion experience in 2002 and was praying intently to be able to see things with Jesus's eyes. The next morning I walked into my medical office and there was a gift basket containing *A Course in Miracles* on my desk. I glanced at the contents and fell speechless into the chair.

The whole purpose of this book is to practically, step by step, help you to literally develop the vision of Christ. Needless to say, it was the right time at my right place, on my narrow road.

In my opinion, this book could not have been written without supernatural help which Mrs. Schucman fully acknowledged. However, I do not believe it is appropriate or even necessary for most people. I have told you earlier that intellectualization (over-thinking) can be a delaying tactic for many in surrendering their illusions of control. This book is very cerebral - at least, the text portion is.

The late Scott Peck, M.D., felt *A Course in Miracles* was incomplete due to its lack of acknowledgment of evil. I think that may be a valid criticism. The Course does warn you of the real possibility of mental disorientation. This is caused by sudden shifts in "levels" of consciousness. Vivid and, at times, startling dreams can be produced in the reader of this work. Overall, I am grateful for the authors' arduous work. (It was seven years in the making.) My advice to those who are interested would be to become part of a small study group and try it. I do not think the reading should be undertaken casually.

If you are interested in pursuing in more depth the underpinnings of your behavior, beyond the standard texts of medical physiology, I highly recommend Robert Sapolsky's *Biology and Human*

Behavior. But remember, I do not think you can define who you are by your body's biology. You are not restricted to it . I believe you and I can rise above our flesh by raising our consciousness. That, in fact, is what I believe to be the narrow road Jesus speaks of.

Life is full of seeming paradoxes, They can be frustrating or they can be liberating. I can almost guarantee they will be frustrating to begin with and that is not a bad sign. I become a little wary around somebody who has it all figured out. I suggest you do so as well. Jesus warned us about these wolves in sheep's clothing. Perhaps the biggest paradox of life revolves around the issue of fear. Jesus tells us, "fear not," yet we are told that wisdom begins with the fear of the Lord. I can try to explain away this language, but at some point I have to admit that it is a paradox that you and I must grow comfortable with. By accepting this paradox, I have found myself strangely less fearful. Remember in Chapter Four, I said I had been afraid all my life. Oddly, I find these fears slowly receding as I embrace the mystery of grace which is a huge paradox itself. The Creator of the universe loved and loves each of us equally and he "wills" that we know Him through His Son. The Holy Spirit was, and is, given freely to all who desire Him. Paradoxically, He creates the desire as well as meets the desire in your and my heart. That is unfathomable and paradoxical, and that is grace. As I awaken to the grace, I am becoming less fearful.

If you recall, I said that Buddhism had, for me, several valuable lessons, especially Zen Buddhism. I think it can help you with the mental process of embracing paradox. It is good practice. It can help you to think non-linearly and move beyond logic or common sense. Christianity, at its heart, is anything but common sense.

If you already enjoy Koan riddles and such, I would invite you to read a Zen master in Christianity, Meister Eckhart. Although his name may not be familiar to you, his influence has been wide and deep among some much more recognized Christian saints and secular writers. The list includes such persons as Julian of Norwich, Teresa of Avila, Martin Luther, St. John of the Cross, Erich Fromm, Thomas Merton, Ernst Block, Saul Bellow, John Updike, Annie Dillard and Carl Jung, just to name a few. This rather obscure 13th century monk wrote his sermons in German vernacular. They are available in a modern English translation titled *Breakthrough*, edited by Matthew Fox. I review his sermons every few years just to give my brain a good dusting. It helps me to move beyond my conscious thoughts into the other Mind I referred to earlier.

You and I are traveling toward the same goal, but the road we each travel on is different. My particular fears are not your particular fears. The last words the Buddha was said to have spoken were, "Work out your salvation with diligence." The apostle Paul wrote, "Work out your salvation with fear and trembling." I say you are capable of being saved from the idea that you have to be sick and in pain. I am saying that, ultimately, only salvation can be said to heal. It will result in a renewing of your mind and that generally leads to a healing of the body. The bridge that connects the salvation to healing is a forgiving heart.

We are all going to walk a road in our lives. One is indeed straight and narrow and it leads to life. Although the way is tiring and, yes, even scary, you are guaranteed to ultimately reach the goal. Not because of your abilities and skill but because the builder of the road has sent the foreman to help you along the way. The seemingly easier, common-sense path that most choose to take also comes with a guarantee. The fine print on its road sign is very hard to read. I can read the fine print because I have spent so much time on this wandering road. It says, "Seek and do not find." Although this wide avenue has many lanes which appear different, it is still the same wide, crooked and, yes, even appealing, dead-end, no- outlet boulevard. I told Chad, Nickie, Kirk, Melanie,

Maria, Ron, Bob and Tom, and I am telling you, that as much as I would like to at times, I cannot walk your particular narrow road. Even if you had an identical twin sibling, he or she will not travel the exact same path. That is what makes it all so interesting.

Looking back, I could go on and on about the different events and books and people that have helped me on my way, but, ultimately, it would not mean a thing for you. We each have our own melodrama to act out. Shakespeare was right. Dr. Libet's experiment was correct. In the big picture, somebody else is in charge of the play's ending. I will play my role, you will play yours. I cannot wake you from your fearful dream, you cannot wake me from mine. But there is Someone who can, if you will but let Him. The choice is yours.